GRIEF AND RENEWAL

DON MIGUEL RUIZ
BARBARA EMRYS

Grief and Renewal

Finding Beauty and Balance in Loss

Urano
publishing

Argentina - Chile - Colombia - Spain
USA - Mexico - Peru - Uruguay

The first edition of this book was published in september 2023

ISBN: 978-1- 953027-09-2

E-ISBN: 978-1-953027-14-6

Printed in Colombia

Library of Cataloging-in-Publication Data

Ruiz, Miguel Angel and Emrys, Barbara

1. Self-Help   2. Spiritual

Grief and Renewal

Index

Orientation Day   9

Day 1: The Reality   19

Day 2: The Reflection   41

Day 3: Grief   71

Day 4: Grace   95

Day 5: The Elegy   125

Orientation Day

Hello and welcome!

Today, we begin a new course in our Mystery School series, where we'll discuss the topic of death and loss in the human experience. This week, we'll consider many points of view about death, while exploring ways to avoid harming ourselves in the wake of loss.

Grief describes the way most of us respond to loss. We naturally grieve over the loss of anything or anyone when there is a strong emotional attachment. How we grieve determines our health and happiness in future days. It affects the relationships that we have with ourselves, with the people we love, and with life itself.

Whoever you are and wherever you're from, you know what grief feels like. Every culture has its own traditions regarding death and loss, but every individual expresses grief differently. Most of us are aware that grieving can heal us. Or, if we let it linger too long, it can cripple us. It can move us through our pain, or it can take us hostage for a lifetime. Grief can inspire us to rise to our greatest heights. It can also defeat us.

Your mind, like everyone's, resists confronting the reality of death. Yet your mind is essential to the healing process after any tragedy. It can teach you to treasure the memories of those who have died. It may also remind you to be kind to the living.

We all know loss. In the process of growing up, we outgrew many beliefs and behaviors. We also needed to abandon outdated ideas about ourselves. We had to give up beloved possessions. And, yes, we had to say goodbye to close friends, sweethearts and precious family members.

We know loss. We also know the fear of losing people we love. The death of someone dear to us is heartbreaking and confusing, but it can reveal some basic truths about ourselves. It can teach us how to live richer lives, having survived a transformational change.

The legacy of a loved one endures through our memories of them. We can use memories to lift ourselves out of darkness, or to invite darkness in. We can use someone's passing as an excuse to suffer, or to rediscover the wonders of living.

In the course of a lifetime, we're likely to experience many deaths and different degrees of loss. We grieve over the loss of our youth and beauty. With age, we lose strengths we took for granted. At any age, we may mourn the loss of a healthy body or a sound mind. We may have our social status taken from us. We may lose our sense of security, or of identity. And we sometimes feel like we've lost ourselves.

We all want to be safe, and any loss—or even the threat of loss—can feel terrifying. Feeling that life has betrayed us, we can allow bitterness to turn us into someone else, something else. The way toward overcoming our grief may seem like a mystery... until we find new insights.

By now, you know this. You've been confronting mysteries all your life. Through your physical birth, you arrived into a world of mysteries. In the earliest months and years of your existence, you explored life's marvels with uninhibited joy. You were hungry to learn and every aspect of your life was a puzzle waiting to be solved.

You lacked the knowledge to explain things back then, but that didn't diminish your enthusiasm. As soon as you could speak, you began asking questions and digging for answers. And you found that symbols were the key to solving the greatest puzzles.

Numbers, letters, simple illustrations… all these helped you in your efforts to understand and communicate. Language was your intellectual challenge. Language was also your greatest artistic tool.

With new information, came knowledge. As knowledge became more familiar, your skills improved. Your wisdom expanded. And, with every mystery you solved, many more mysteries revealed themselves.

Your life is your art, so remember to approach every lesson from the point of view of an artist. You've learned so much and you've put what you learned into practice; the result is that your art has become more interesting and complex.

Do you see how surviving a devastating loss is another of life's countless artistic challenges? You can use these simple reminders to help you meet those challenges:

See. Like any good artist, your challenge is to see everything, however pleasant or unpleasant. Being able to see things as they are is the essence of awareness. Seeing, without bias, strengthens your faith in yourself.

Feel. Allow yourself to feel to the fullest, no matter how tender or terrible the emotion seems to you. Turn tragedy into poetry. Turn despair into creativity. To protect your own masterpiece, turn sorrow into a celebration.

Say no to your stories. Your thoughts can take you down painful pathways, or direct your attention to the present moment. They can encourage self-pity or they can come to your rescue when events seem challenging. Most thoughts don't come in whispers. They pound through you, screaming loudly and bringing with them a torrent of emotions. Stop what you're doing! they scream. Hear us! Believe us! Die for us!

For this reason, your thoughts shouldn't be a mystery to you. It's easy to hear what you're telling yourself. You're able to listen and you're able to learn. Like life, you can change and modify, even in the process of creating.

Say yes to life. Accept all of life's surprises. Say yes to life's unpredictability. Say yes to its endless possibilities.

Say yes, because life is the supreme artist, teaching you to create something beautiful out of every circumstance.

Your existence is defined by a constant stream of events. Some events may seem tragic, some exhilarating. Either way, events keep happening. The way you respond is usually reflexive; but you can choose to respond consciously. You can respond to life as a master artist would.

For instance, you can recognize yourself as an active collaborator with life. You can sharpen your eye for beauty. You can lessen your judgments and open yourself to change. You can dare to see things as they are.

You can also be kinder to your body, and acknowledge it as a loyal friend. In truth, your body is more than just a friend. It is the love of your life. Has anyone ever been more intimately connected to you than your physical body?

Has anyone supported you more, through good times and bad, through sickness and health? Has anyone been more willing to serve your best and worst impulses, or to assist you in achieving your ambitions? It's doubtful that anyone has taken as much poison from you, without resentment or blame.

It's not too late to show your body the unconditional love it deserves. It's never too late to be a devoted caretaker to this human being. Respecting the body is the most essential part of mastering life.

Most of us are inattentive to our bodies until they give us trouble. And, when that happens, we tend to be resentful. In most cases, we blame the "animal" for the inconvenience it's caused us. We're impatient and critical.

We see everything from the perspective of the mind, which is not always sympathetic toward the human being. We're mind-drunk, and so mesmerized by our thoughts that we can't see the wonder that exists beyond them.

We all have the choice to get out of our heads and make ourselves available to happiness. We can engage with people close to us. We can accept the love that's offered to us, and dare to give love in return. We can allow our hearts to open wide, and then wider still.

Given a chance, our physical bodies will find the strength to lift us into sunlight and keep us there. We can be patient, as we begin to apply our art once again. We can pick and choose what to believe, as all the pieces of us rise from the ruins of a broken dream.

As I've said, one of the many consequences of losing someone is losing yourself. It's easy to neglect the needs of the body in times of grief. It's easy, when sorrow is so heavy in you, to collapse under the weight of it. You can ignore all the familiar paths to joy and refuse the little pleasures that make life worth experiencing.

In the midst of trauma, or in the aftermath of an unexpected loss, self-pity can defeat you. Guilt or shame may seem to overwhelm you. Yes, you may lose touch with yourself, putting your loyalty to the dead ahead of your duty to the living.

If any of this sounds familiar, you may be ready for deeper insights. If you think death took everything wonderful from you, I assure you that more wonders are waiting. Life is calling you back to its never-ending game of mysteries.

Are you still willing to play?

Day 1:
The
Reality

Holding a hand up to his eyes,
he realized
that he, too, was made of the seen and unseen. . .
those million stars
and the space between!

Good morning and welcome back!

Today, I'll begin with the story of a medicine man who lived long, long ago. But, like most timeless stories, this one is also about you, me and our natural desire to seek the truth.

This man, though still young, had dedicated his life in search of truth. Feeling there was more to being a great shaman than he'd learned from his ancestral teachings, he was hungry for new revelations. So, he left the village one night and made his way to the high desert, to find a quiet place to meditate.

As the sun set behind the western mountains, he found a secluded spot and made camp. He ate a modest meal, and very quickly fell asleep under the night sky.

It was well past midnight when he woke again and found himself gazing up at the heavens. There was no moon that night, and the stars were bright. Each speck of light blazed like a diamond against the blackness of space. Stars... and the vast, empty space between the stars.

As the young man raised a hand to rub his tired eyes he noticed his fingers outlined against the brilliant sky. As he looked, it seemed he was seeing through his hand, to the stars beyond. Or, could it be that his hands, too, were made of stars?

In that instant, he felt as if he was waking from a lifetime of sleep. He rose to his feet, looked down at his body, and then up at the night sky. A smile of comprehension lit his face. "I am made of stars... and the space between stars," he said to himself.

While he processed that thought, it also occurred to him that the stars didn't create light, as he'd assumed. Light created the stars. "My entire body is made of light," he whispered. "Everything is made of light!"

He saw that the space between stars was not empty, but filled with light. Light, he realized, contained all the information of life. His body, like all bodies, was indeed made of stars. All matter was made of atoms and the brilliant space between.

The universe is made of matter and the creative force of energy that makes life possible. This force was the truth of him. It is the truth of all living beings.

That night, in a sudden moment of inspiration, the medicine man saw himself in everything. He saw himself in every human, animal, insect, and tree. He saw himself in the forests, oceans, and meadows. He saw himself in clouds, in rain, and in the earth under his feet. He saw how life combined matter and energy to create countless manifestations of itself.

"I am life!" he shouted to the glittering sky. "And I see myself reflected in every human being!" It was suddenly obvious that people were mirrors for each other, but a kind of smoke blurred their vision. It obscured the truth from them.

"Ah!" he exclaimed. "The mirror is the dreamer, the mind of every human being… and the smoke is the dream itself!"

As Above, So Below

The man standing beneath the stars could see that his body was a copy of the heavens. It was made of particles of matter, as well as the mystery that lay between the particles.

He was made of flesh, yes. He was made of matter, and also the invisible force that moved matter. He was the energy that sustained his human body throughout its years of existence and would someday reclaim it.

The young shaman in this story suddenly saw the bigger picture. You could say he saw the biggest picture possible. Like him, we can gain wisdom and perspective by expanding our awareness. We can look up to the heavens, or inward to the simplest component of our bodies, and see life.

There is only one true perspective: life's perspective. It perceives itself through every object and being. Life is all there is.

This realization changes the way we see ourselves and everyone else. It may someday transform the way all humans view the world. Most of us imagine very little beyond our own versions of reality. We have opinions about what we see, and we make all-important decisions based on those opinions. Opinions, however, are not truth. Opinions are stories we tell about truth.

Like the medicine man in this story, we hardly take a moment to consider the big picture. But, during that moonless night in the desert, he finally realized how he'd been misled by the familiar stories of his youth. He saw how knowledge, for all its wonders, was the smoke that dimmed human awareness.

This insight changed him forever. And, to ensure that he never forgot the lessons he learned that night, he gave himself a new name. He would call himself Smoky Mirror.

In every moment, we humans can make the choice to be more aware. We can broaden our point of view, or we can balance many points of view. We can open our eyes to the biggest possible picture, as Smoky Mirror dared to do.

Every mind is a mirror, reflecting the physical world; but mirrors also distort what they reflect. How well is your mind doing its job? Is it ready to get out of its own way? Is it ready to put knowledge into perspective, and to see life as it is?

The story of Smoky Mirror is a simple lesson in awareness. It reminds us how, even in adulthood, we're willing to believe whatever we're told. It calls us to leave innocence behind, and begin to see things as they are.

Our stories try to explain truth, but often take us farther away from it. Fear distorts the way we perceive everything around us; and, of course, fear distorts the way we perceive ourselves. Transfixed by our version of reality, we imagine that life is separate from us, and maybe even hostile toward us.

Human existence brings turmoil, tranquility, and all probabilities at once. It includes all outcomes and expressions, simultaneously. Your life is a comedy and a tragedy. Your stories are not the truth; too often, they refuse to acknowledge the truth.

We are members of a specific species, existing on one planet among many planets within one of countless solar systems... within the only universe we know. None of that makes us small or ordinary. All forms of life, known or unknown, are extraordinary. Every being is a miracle of creation.

Every life-form has unique characteristics. Each has a distinctive talent and each makes its own contributions to life as a whole. However, no creature is immortal. Whatever our function, we're all made of matter. And matter doesn't last forever.

Truth does, however, and truth is the essence of you.

The Balance

Something dies and something else is born, continuously. Matter exists in one form, and then rearranges itself into another form. Or, it ceases to exist as matter. Life is the perpetual process of creation and destruction. The result, whether we choose to see it or not, is perfect balance.

We humans are born, we live and we die. While we live, our actions reflect life's process. We are created; in turn, we create. We witness many births and many kinds of deaths, but it's not always easy for us to see the balance.

Most of us react badly to loss. To infinite life, however, nothing is lost and nothing is gained. Do you suppose that life regrets a single act of destruction or creation? Does it regret having made mortal stuff—a tree, a bird, a person? Does life stop creating because of the tragedy of broken things?

Life is transforming matter all the time. You could say it transforms the mirror, which is your body, and all living bodies. You, in turn, are transforming the mirror's reflection, which is your mind.

Your mind uses language to create a word-picture of everything the physical body is experiencing. Your brain gathers information, and your mind reflects that information through ideas. That's the mind's function, and also its art.

With every shift in perception, with every new realization, the reflection becomes clearer. Your art gets better. I think you'll agree that great art reflects life well. You're in charge of what you believe, so you can direct your attention as any artist would, with an eye for beauty and a desire for truth.

As your mind evolves, it can learn to reflect life more accurately, more honestly. For that to start happening, it must believe its own stories less and to trust life much more. Let's see what that implies.

So many of our shared stories are about death and loss. We're afraid of losing the people we love or the objects we value. We're afraid of losing our familiar ways of thinking and believing. Beyond that, we're afraid of feeling unsafe.

We don't feel safe when our normal reality is disrupted. The thought of losing something is enough to cause us fear, and fear then drives our decision-making. It guides our actions. It lies at the heart of our storytelling.

We know our lives will end, and yet we fight the reality of death. When something dear to us is lost, we tell ourselves that the god we worship doesn't love us or that life is unfair. We see misfortune as a punishment; we assume that tragedy only strikes those who don't deserve to prosper and be happy.

But death doesn't discriminate. It touches everyone. Life doesn't discriminate; everything that exists is the result of life's creative process. Loss is an inevitable part of that process. As artists, we could easily appreciate the beauty and balance of death, if we weren't taking it all so personally.

Yes, there's perfect balance in creation. In fact, the way life corrects imbalance is amazing; but, to us, it can look violent, even catastrophic. Everything looks different from the point of view of the mind.

Your mind is a function of your brain and, like the rest of your body, your brain is made of matter. It will last only as long as your physical body does. Even so, the mind likes to tell a different story.

The mind can process any number of complex philosophies; but clearly, it resists the idea of its own death. It sees it as an impossibility, and imagines it will live on forever, even without the body.

An aware mind sees itself more clearly however. It can admit to its role as a storyteller. It can see itself as an artist and creator, reflecting life as clearly as it knows how. It can recognize its own quirks and limitations. And it can accept its own mortality.

As we'll see later in the week, your mind is even capable of creating its own kind of balance by building something rewarding out of trauma and loss.

Immortals

Remember the story about the single sperm that wins the race to create a human being? One little guy was able to fertilize an egg, in spite of the sixty-or-so million others that were sent to do the job in the same instant.

Well, there's another side to that story. It's about the many millions that didn't succeed in their mission. It's about all the sperm that died while trying to create life. That part of the story unfolds every time you make love. It happens whenever creatures mate, which means it's happening in real time, all the time.

For every spermatozoon winning the biological lottery, there are countless millions sacrificing themselves. Does that sound like a tragedy to you? If so, then it's the original tragedy. Every tragedy ever told was born from this.

Of course, I'm only illustrating the process of creation, which shouldn't be seen as tragic. It's a tragedy to lose the people who gave our lives pleasure and meaning. The loss of a human being may seem disastrous to us, but loss is basic to creation.

Life is the one creative force. It has no story and no main character. Life is limitless energy, and energy has no personal agenda. Life is truth, and truth has no motive.

Creating involves disturbance, if not violent change. What once existed is altered or destroyed, and it's safe to say that life doesn't care. Life's reflection, on the other hand, cares very much.

You care. Most people care. To care is normal for human beings. To get caught up in your own drama is normal. But caring doesn't mean it's necessary to cause yourself harm. And, what you believe about caring, or about human drama, could actually hurt you.

Maybe you care about your physical body, and try to spare it unnecessary emotional pain. At the same time, you care so much about the judgments of other people that you're willing to experience the pain over and over. You may say you don't want to destroy yourself, yet you seem willing to die, in little stages, from your own regrets and recriminations.

So, be aware of the crimes you commit against yourself, many of them in the name of caring. Even as a rational adult, you find excuses to hurt yourself. You find so many reasons to suffer.

Obeying spiritual laws, you may deprive yourself of food and sleep. You might support habits and principles that go against your natural instincts. You could be following advice that puts your relationships at risk, or ideologies that put lives at risk.

And you've learned the habit of hurting yourself in response to a loss. The end of a love affair can be your excuse to punish yourself; it may even seem reasonable to judge yourself a thousand times over. The end of a career or a business investment may affect you in the same way.

You may even turn against yourself at the thought of a damaged reputation or the idea of a public humiliation. It's possible that you use people and circumstances as excuses to hurt yourself on a regular basis.

Like most people, you've probably beaten yourself up over many small disappointments and imagined failures. Haven't you ever seen love as an excuse to reject yourself, or to let a heartbreak continue for years? We humans corrupt love by using it against ourselves, but love isn't our only justification for pain.

We frequently use success as a reason to feel guilty. We use praise as a reason to feel unworthy. We use the idea of a divine being to ignite fear and hatred. We fight each other over our individual definitions of truth. And, of course, we use our fear of death as an excuse not to live a productive and happy life.

It's fair to say that most of us struggle against the idea of old age and death. We hurt ourselves by resisting what is inevitable, even beautiful. We're hungry for stories about ordinary people becoming superhuman, indestructible. We want to believe in gods, demi-gods, and immortal beings.

We might also want to consider the wonders of being mortal. It may be that, even when we imagine ourselves as the superior species, we're still not getting a clear picture of how extraordinary we are—just the way we are.

Heart and Soul

Until now, you've probably had no reason to doubt your thoughts. Knowledge tells you what to believe or not believe, but knowledge is not what you are. You're not the sum of what you know. You're not your remembered experiences. And, you're not the character you created and call "me", with its long history and colorful personality.

Me isn't the truth of you. It's a fanciful reflection of the truth. Your mind reflects life through stories, and the main character of your particular story is whoever you describe yourself to be.

Me is an essential part of your art, and art is always evolving. Life is constantly changing matter, just as you change truth's reflection. Life is the master artist and you are its student. As you grow in awareness, you become a master for others.

Yes, you become a teacher to those who can learn from you. Even in grieving, you have something to teach. As you challenge your own fears around death, you modify humanity's fear. As you challenge your own attitudes about loss, you become a source of strength for everyone you know.

Smoky Mirror went home to his village to share his insights with those who would listen. He was a teacher, sharing his point of view with the world. So are you. You teach yourself, your friends, your coworkers. You teach your children and their children.

At this moment, there are billions of humans teaching other humans. There are humans informing other species and other species informing humans. Every creature is born learning the ways of its species; every creature will pass that information on to the next generation. Each is reflecting life in a unique way.

Life teaches matter to be a better mirror, to reflect truth more accurately. It teaches all creatures to benefit from the experience of being alive, and to share what they've learned, however they can.

For every living thing, learning starts in infancy and ends when the physical body dies. If you understand this, you understand that life is still teaching you. Life will never stop guiding your evolution.

You're made of matter, yes; but you're also the energy that creates matter. The collaboration of energy and matter produces countless different life forms. Each has its own way of perceiving, and each mirrors life.

All creatures function in ways that make them well-suited to their environments. As I said, no life is more or less valuable than another; but, it seems that humans prefer to think of themselves as superior to all other forms of life.

We have different talents, for sure. We have the ability to think. We can imagine… we can remember the past and foresee a future. Regardless of whether or not these skills are unique to us, they're amazing. But thinking is supposed to help us create. Too often we use that unique talent to cause ourselves confusion and pain.

Like a warped mirror casts a corrupted image, thinking can corrupt our most benevolent intentions. Ideologies turn us against ourselves and superstitions turn us against our own kind.

We use words as weapons, even words that should give us comfort. Words like love and truth are synonymous with life itself. And yet, in many ways, we use them against life. We use them to create conflict. We use them to do ourselves harm.

In too many cases, we use language, our greatest art, to cause fear and division. We use words as weapons against each other. We tell terrifying stories about the word death. We tell disheartening stories about the word love.

"Love hurts," we say. "Love is madness. To love is to submit to insanity." Many think of love as a weakness. It's seen as a challenge; one that's much too difficult to meet. They think of it as a single emotion, but love is the force of life itself. It's the force that created you and it guides you through the challenges of a normal day.

The word truth is interpreted differently by every individual. We tend to think of truth as a relative thing, rather than the only thing. Life is truth. Our stories and opinions about life are not.

And we misinterpret the idea of a soul. "I love you, with all my heart and soul," is a profound thing to say to someone; you and I can agree on that. The heart symbolizes the strength and depth of our emotions, after all. But why do we talk about "killing" the soul, or "stealing" it?

The soul is not made of matter. The soul is a force of life. It isn't something that can be corrupted or defeated. It can't be diminished or compromised. The word soul is best defined as the force that recognizes every particle within a single universe.

One such universe is your body, and any outside trespass is unwelcome. Any foreign substance is attacked and rejected. You witness that defensive reaction whenever you get a splinter, or contract a virus. And, without anti-rejection medications, an organ transplant will fail.

The soul is energy, supporting the integrity of matter while it exists. Matter is a dance of particles and space. Matter is formless, insubstantial; and yet something makes it appear to have shape and form.

Your soul is that something, holding all the particles of matter together. By mentioning the soul, you acknowledge the part of you that is unseen and mysterious. By invoking the soul, you're calling attention to your divinity.

The main character of your story is a myth; it has no afterlife. Your physical body, too, is temporal. But life will always renew itself through the interaction of energy and matter. Life will forever reincarnate. That's the big picture.

How does seeing the big picture help to heal us, especially after a devastating loss? Well, it's important to remind ourselves that life is forever in the act of creating. In the process, much appears to be gained and much seems to be lost, and yet the result is total equilibrium. In the big picture, there is only balance.

The exchange of information between energy and matter is ongoing, resulting in more and more life.

You are life. You are made of the same eternal energy that creates worlds, and energy never ends.

You are the power of life in action. Keeping that in mind, perhaps you have a better understanding of what it means to believe in yourself. Faith in you is the realization that you are every part of life's equation. You are all things at once.

You are life and death. You are energy and matter, and the ongoing dance between the two. Hold that image as you fall into sleep tonight. Tomorrow, I'll ask you to remember how life works, and to consider how life's reflection works.

Your body is an organism made of matter and energy. It's made of real things. It's an exact copy of the truth. When I refer to reflection, I'm talking about your mind. When I refer to your mind, I'm talking about a storyteller. I'm talking about the unreal and unreliable mirror image of the truth.

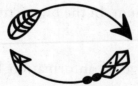

Day 2:
The Reflection

Images of beauty you'll never find
in muddied ponds—brackish, brined—
but only in the clear, reflective kind.

Hello and welcome again!

As you know, we're here to explore ways to survive a painful loss without doing ourselves harm. We want to discover how our approach to death can inspire a more conscious approach to living.

It was important, on our first day, to see how life works. Life is constantly creating more life and creation requires dynamic change and upheaval, as we can see by observing our planet and the surrounding cosmos.

The creation of our solar system as it exists today involved cataclysmic events that have gone on for billions of years. These events will continue without end. And we're talking about just one planetary system among countless others, in a universe that is too vast to fully understand.

Smoky Mirror, an instinctive scientist, saw that light exists everywhere. You and I are made of light, and we reflect light. We reflect light in obvious ways, and also in subtle ways… in ways we rarely consider.

Our stories attempt to reflect the truth, but they are not the truth. As you listen to these words right now, you're focusing on their meaning, right? Imagine all the neurological functions that must work well in order for you to find meaning in what you hear. We reflect light in subtle ways…

Imagine your brain, your mind, and your nervous system working together to makes sense of my words. Imagine, now, turning them into your own story, theory, and revelation. This is your genius. This is your art.

You perceive and shape perceptions into thoughts. Try to imagine the tasks your body is performing now, while you sit very still. Maybe you can feel the miracles taking place that make comprehension possible. You might feel thoughts being weighed and processed.

Beyond the thoughts and theories, you may sense something else. You may sense what is real about you, like the blood pulsing through your veins and an electric current coursing through your nervous system.

Move your attention outward, and sense the room around you. Acknowledge the objects that fill it and the space between those objects. Rather than seeing it all, try to feel it all.

Now feel the whole building, or house, you occupy. Feel the neighborhood that stretches beyond it. Then get a sense of Earth's countless creatures going about their lives—working, creating, and surviving, just as you're doing.

Imagine the continental mass that lies beneath everything. Imagine the entire surface of this planet; and then imagine the planet moving you through space.

Expand your senses outward and envision this planet's solar system, the galaxy that embraces it, and the countless galaxies beyond.

Your mind may not have a clear image of this universe, or other unexplored universes, but you can now begin to sense the infinite nature of life. You can sense what is true.

You can sense life's unstoppable creative force. On some level, you're aware of the power of energy itself. There, in that awareness, is where I'd like us to begin our conversation about death and loss.

Retelling the Story

The story of Smoky Mirror is a tribute to the creative power that surges through every living thing. Life is the architect and creator of everything you see and experience. Like clay in the hands of a sculptor, matter is an ever-changing piece of art.

Your human body is made of matter, of atoms and molecules. You are an evolving piece of art. Through thoughts and ideas, your mind mirrors the physical world. It structures its own version of reality by telling a convincing story. And, yes, it evolves; not according to life's blueprint, but according to your will.

Your mind converts what is real into symbols: words, thoughts, and mental images. It turns real life into something virtual. It magically turns perception into a narrative, and you can direct that narrative.

Like the mirror it is, the mind reflects the physical world as well as it can. How well it does so depends on the materials available to it, meaning the information at hand and the brain's ability to process that information.

Telling a story about everything perceived is an amazing neurological achievement. It's astonishing, but it can also cause serious problems. Every mind accepts its version of reality as truth. And, since every mind sees reality a little differently, this can lead to conflict.

Most of us feel safer when we're certain. And we want other people to be certain of us, too. We're reluctant to say things like, "I can't be sure what I'm about to say is true, but…," or even to add a simple disclaimer like, "This is just my own interpretation of events." We don't want to admit we're guessing.

In fact, most of us invest total faith in an idea, regardless of the consequences. We commit to our version of the truth at all costs. To do less would challenge the beliefs that support our reality. It would make us feel unsafe.

There's nothing right or wrong about any of this. As life creates, so do we all create. But it helps us to see how our minds work. When we see that we're designing our own reflection of what is real, we can modify the way we do it. We can alter the reflection itself. We can mirror life more accurately, if not perfectly.

As I say, the mind is amazing. Making a story out of the information we get from life is genius. Learning to modify that story is a big step forward in awareness. Not believing your story, or anyone's story, can be called transcendence.

Transcending your own knowledge is a mastery. Like a master artist, you can learn to represent life in the simplest and most authentic way possible. You don't have to make assumptions. You can do away with expectations. You can demand nothing more from life than what it offers, and give no more than your capabilities allow.

You can be such a master. Your mind can evaluate its stories. It can "listen" to its own thoughts. It can decide how well its conclusions faithfully represent reality. It can form a conscious collaboration with the physical body, which will benefit your entire world.

Until now, your body has been a servant to your thoughts. Your mind has played the role of a tyrant most of your life. It frequently judges and punishes your body for its inadequacies. But so-called flaws and failures are just part of a story built on opinions.

The human mind shouldn't use its amazing abilities to judge, to blame, or to berate the body; and yet, that's what we've encouraged our minds to do since we learned to think. Listen to the way you shape opinions about yourself. So many of your beliefs are based on disrespect for the physical body.

"I'm only human," is an interesting phrase. The human isn't saying it; knowledge is. It's claiming that humans have major defects. It's suggesting that being human is demeaning and shameful. And yet, without the human there is no thought, no access to knowledge. Without the human, there is no story and no storyteller.

We deliver insults and casual condemnations to our bodies all the time. We judge the bodies around us. We turn our judgments into acts of cruelty. We do these things routinely and we rarely stop to wonder why.

Your mind lives in its own story. Your body responds chemically and emotionally to that story. It responds to every thought and every conversation, spoken or unspoken. But your mind can also admit to its own bullying and make changes.

Your mind can finally learn to serve the human body. After all, hasn't your body spent a lifetime serving you? Hasn't it supported your irrational beliefs and opinions? Hasn't it fed you the emotions you crave? Hasn't done everything it can to heal itself without the mind's interference?

Your mind can see itself, hear itself, and make corrections. It can choose to be a better caretaker. It can yield its own desires to the needs of the body. It can learn the language of kindness and gratitude.

Your mind can imagine truth differently. It can accept love as the power of life itself, not as a game or as a weapon. It can surrender to that power; it can serve life, not just a system of beliefs. And, in serving life, it can graciously accept the idea of death.

An aware mind does all of this.

The Voice and Me

Life is all that exists. Life, or pure energy, creates matter. Think of a particle of light as the initial building block of matter. It's a block, or a brick, initiating the structure that is the manifest world. Light builds a universe of visible things.

Without light, there would be no world to see, nor would we have the ability to see it. Light is everywhere, as the young shaman realized that night in the desert. Light is never absent. So, what is shadow?

A shadow occurs when light is obstructed. For instance, your body casts a shadow on the ground between you and the sun's rays. And you can count on a big, leafy tree to offer relief from the heat of the sun.

You also know that when our planet is situated between the moon and the sun, you can see its shadow cross the face of the moon. You've seen eclipses, and you understand what makes them happen. So, you know that shadow is not the absence of light; it's only the lessening of light's intensity.

Now think of awareness as the sun's light. Imagine yourself standing in the way of that. Your knowledge can, and often does, lessen the intensity of awareness. Much of what you believe inhibits your ability to see.

It's hard to comprehend anything when you refuse to be informed. It's difficult to find enlightenment when you're living deep in the shadow of your own stories. You may find you've been inviting this sort of darkness, even though life offers you countless different ways to perceive the world.

It's up to you to make an effort to see what really exists. Be fearless in your seeing. See the force of life in all things. See below the surface, to the depths of you. There is only life: surging, slowing, and surging again.

Be patient as you learn to be more aware. When you find yourself struggling against life's amazing current, let go. Surrender to it. That unstoppable current is the truth of you.

The voice of me, the character you created, is a product your social programming. You know this voice. It speaks through your conversations with others and your silent communications with yourself. It tells stories to teach and entertain other people. It tells an ongoing story to itself. It narrates the ongoing events of your life.

It explains what the body is feeling, as well as what's going on in the world outside. What you know informs your conversations. What you know inspires your emotional and physical reactions. Me, then, is the voice of knowledge.

At a time when you knew nothing, you had to believe everything people said; and what they said about you, in particular, stayed in your mind. Your self-image has been influenced by many people in your life, especially the people who raised you.

You have a story. Call it a thought process or a memory. Call it a belief system. The story has a central character, and this character has a voice. It runs in your head as random thoughts and imagined conversations. It expresses itself in your spoken conversations and long-held beliefs.

Our minds contain a library of knowledge, based on our education and personal experiences. Knowledge can inform and inspire us. It can lift us out of fear and ignorance. Knowledge is an amazing tool for human communication; but knowledge isn't the same as truth.

Knowledge, for all its gifts, is also the chief reason we suffer. The voice in our head is not always the voice of a friend. It may not provide much comfort in difficult situations; in fact, it can often seem hostile. The main character of your story can sometimes sound like your worst enemy.

The character you created is not an entity separate from you. The voice that whispers in your head is your own. Do you still agree with what it says and believes? Does it continue to represent the person you think you are?

We all talk to ourselves. We tell ourselves what's going on before we tell anybody else, and our bodies get the message right away. But, do we pay attention to what we're saying? Do we question our own version of events or do we try to save the nervous system from unnecessary distress?

Observe how faithfully your emotions obey the mind's narrative. In most cases, you get upset without knowing why. Listen to the quiet messages you deliver to yourself and decide if you want to communicate differently.

Agree to be skeptical of your own voice. You can't be at peace as long as your mind is at war with itself. You won't find clarity when you deny yourself information. See that, and let in some light.

You can't heal from a traumatic event if you're adding to the trauma. Your mental narrative shouldn't be causing you more stress. Accusing yourself, blaming yourself, only makes the emotional pain worse. It's important to see what you do to yourself in times of grief and trauma, and to make adjustments.

See, without having to interpret what you see. Feel, without telling yourself how to feel. Your mind and body need to develop a relationship based on trust. The problem is, few of us were taught how to do that.

If you listen closely, you can hear your own mind at war. Your attention is torn between many conflicting ideas. You struggle with concepts of right and wrong. You argue with yourself and you blame yourself. You scold yourself. And the body pays a price.

Your mind has always imagined itself to be the master of your physical body. And by now, your body is resigned to being a servant to your stories. This, as you might guess, isn't the formula for a good relationship of any kind.

Mutual respect creates balance in any relationship. Honest communication helps heal wounds. Listen to the language of your thoughts, and agree to modify the way you communicate with yourself and others in your dream.

A dysfunctional relationship between your mind and body can do a lot of harm. And that relationship affects your overall health. It also affects people close to you. You can probably see how it might create a disturbance in your entire reality, as well as the reality we all share as humans.

The Storm

Your mind tells stories about you, but the mind isn't you. The hero of your story is an idea, a picture-image, but not what you are. The same is true of your body.

Your body is a biological organism. It allows you to feel, to experience, and to dream; but it's not you. You'll never fully know what you are, which makes you one of life's superb mysteries.

You realize your body is destined to die, but you want to believe the main character will not. Your mind imagines it will survive the body's death, and take all of its knowledge with it, but the mind isn't immortal, nor is the main character of its story.

When your brain dies, your mind's wonderful work is over; but energy is eternal. Life goes on and on. It has no personal agenda and no desires. It has unlimited potential and no story to tell.

While you live as a human being, you have plenty of stories to tell. Every story, every thought, triggers an emotional response, which means the potential for drama is always present. Emotions create a storm front. Thunder rolls and winds shift. The weather can change at any time.

Feelings brew, they spill over, they pull back, and they spill over again… often wreaking havoc on your world. The storm inside of you spreads outward, affecting your most intimate relationships. It affects your work. It affects your ability to function well. We can all see how humanity is affected by the same storm. The storm calms only when each of us takes responsibility for our thoughts and reactions. Think how that would change our view of reality. Think of what that would mean to the collective reality of humans on this planet.

The voice in your head is a constant reminder of what you think you know. It's your mind, talking to itself. This simple realization can help you make important changes in your communication with everyone, most of all with yourself. It gives you power over your own attention. It puts you in charge of your own thoughts.

It's natural to feel the emotional distress of a loss. Your body registers the emotional pain before your mind has a chance to form an opinion about it. Without the angry thoughts or tales of regret you will still feel the anguish. Without other people's emotional input, the shock of losing someone will still hurt you.

So it's important for your mind to accept its role as a caretaker of the body, at all times. It is vital that it guards you in times of shock and grief. It's important that it learn to be the provider of comfort, not the voice of doom.

Peace on this planet begins with your own thought process. It begins when you improve the relationship between mind and body. If you can do that, so can the rest of humanity. It's up to each of us to calm the storm that begins in our own minds.

Blame It On the Stars

How we react to people and events is up to us; but more often than not, we want to blame our behavior on someone else. "He made me so mad," we'll say. "She drove me to it… it's not my fault… they did it first!" Most of us tend to blame other people for the things we do and say. And we blame random things, as well.

We blame circumstances, or the stars. We blame our reckless behavior on an unhappy childhood, or just bad luck. Sadly, we're quick to blame our bodies. We blame the fact that we're "only human."

When we run out of people to blame, we turn to things unseen. We turn to superstition. "The devil made me do it," sounds like a joke, but devils and angels get way too much credit for what we choose to do and say.

Demons put evil thoughts in our heads. Really? Angels toy with us. God judges us and finds us guilty. Is any of this true? It seems we want to believe we're being condemned by someone, somewhere, all the time.

If your thoughts sound demonic to you, that may be because they are. If your inner voice seems to want to hurt you, that may be because it does. It's your voice. These are your thoughts. Again, don't believe them, but listen and learn. Do it because you love yourself.

Listen, learn, and change what you're doing. Your mind stirs up emotions in you all day long. It does this automatically. It does it effortlessly, just by conjuring images that trigger feelings in the body. It plays with pain. It recalls your most distressing thoughts and memories.

Distress could mean sudden anger or a vague sense of anxiety. It could be sadness, joy, or jealousy. Whatever the mood, your emotions are being manipulated. You're being bullied by a voice that's been speaking to you, and for you, nearly all of your life.

No one is forcing you to react to that voice. You just do. This illustrates the relationship most of us have with our minds. We're willing to be victims of our thoughts. You, like everyone, tolerate unnecessary emotional abuses, and you're the only one who can turn that around.

You can do it by changing the way you think and react. You can choose another way of communicating with yourself, starting now. Be the friend and the savior you need, if only for the sake of the body that serves you so well.

Every human reflects life's creative process. You, like life, are constantly creating. You may not think of yourself as an artist or an architect, but you build realities out of what you sense and perceive.

You build narratives out of every physical experience, and many imagined experiences. What you think, you believe. What you believe directs your actions. We all excel at the art of storytelling, but few of us ever doubt our own stories.

We rarely challenge our own beliefs. We rarely ask if what we're thinking is true. We don't consider what motivates our decision-making. We're reluctant to step out of the reality we created.

So many of us are afraid to make the slightest change to our routines. We think that change means loss; and we see any loss as a misfortune. Death is an inevitable part of creation, but we see death as an injustice.

There are ways to honor the ever-changing events in human life without hurting ourselves in the process. We can allow emotions to come and go freely; we can avoid holding on to pain and regret. And we can stop feeding the sorrow that comes from loss.

Notice how you use memory to keep old heartbreaks alive. Recognize it, and agree to not seek out pain. Look at the things, the people, and the events, that tempt you to feel guilty and ashamed. What you see, you can change.

Dreams end so that other dreams may grow. More dreams and more mysteries follow. Look ahead. Remember that you, too, are a creator, and make something new. Reflect life the best way you know how. That could mean accepting loss with grace. It could mean saying yes to situations as they occur.

And it could mean finally making peace with death.

Save the Living

Where once there was nothing, something explodes into existence. It grows, it flourishes, and gradually decays. Something else, somewhere else, is born. All things thrive and reproduce. All things wither and die.

We can all see the beauty of that brief evolution in a flower, or in the lifespan of a butterfly. And yet we find it hard to see the beauty in our own fleeting existence. Still, each of us, including the most fearful among us, has experienced death in many ways.

Growing up requires many changes and the death of many realities. This present moment replaced a past moment, and future moments will replace this one. Every life event causes an upset to body and mind. You know that; you've lived through many such disturbances yourself.

As a child, you were shaken when familiar routines were altered. You were probably upset when you had to move to a new neighborhood, or graduate from one school to enter another. You made friends and lost friends. Cherished expectations were shattered. Emotions may have overwhelmed you, defined you, and then passed out of memory.

As you matured, you saw dreams end. You saw new dreams come into existence and thrive. You invested heavily in a certain view of reality, but eventually your investment weakened and died. As your dreams shifted, you invested again.

People have come and gone in the course of your lifetime. Some were ripped from you, perhaps. Even the strongest bonds were worn away by time. And your physical body felt the force of those bonds, as well as the pain of losing them.

Your body reacts to you, the reflection. Whatever you believe is tragic will be felt with intensity. You form attachments to everything around you—secondary characters, possessions, places, ideas, and relationships. They all end at a certain point. And, if these attachments are strong, you grieve when the bond is broken.

You may even grieve before it breaks; because, like every other human, you've learned to anticipate loss. You've learned to fear the possibility of loss, another habit that takes its toll on your body.

Your body, meanwhile, understands death on its own terms. It experiences countless little deaths, as cells are destroyed and then replaced. It has already experienced huge physical transformations while growing from infancy to childhood, and from childhood to your present state of maturity. It's still changing, and will continue to change and reshape itself.

What the body finds difficult to process are your messages of foreboding. You've been subjecting it to stories that have no basis in reality. You've asked it to react to assumptions and speculations. You've blamed your body for sins it never committed and asked it to pay for your guilt.

Your mind reflects life, however accurately or inaccurately. Your physical body reacts to the outside environment; but it has an equally strong emotional reaction to you, the reflection.

And the reflection doesn't like the idea of death. After the loss of someone near to you, your mind usually finds ways to inflame the wound. Instead, it can save you. Your mind is essential to the process of healing, but it needs to be shown how to be a friend and an ally.

Allow your mind to be a help in your recovery. Allow it to find solutions to problems, which is what it was designed to do. Allow it to cast aside old beliefs for new ones, and then update new opinions when they no longer seem helpful.

From the point of view of energy, there are no endings. There is no death. From the point of view of matter, however, death is all too real. Every loss is tragic, and some tragedies may seem too great to overcome. This can change.

Little changes can be part of your everyday routine. You can change the way you see the people you love, and reconsider the way you approach strangers.

See what lies behind the eyes of another human being. See life, even in death.

You and I are copies of life, made of atoms and unseen energy. Interactions between energy and matter can seem extreme to us; but what appears to have been destroyed has, more accurately, been transformed.

Your mind can learn to find joy in the memory of someone who has died. It can remind you to cherish the living. It can direct its attention toward the bigger picture. That kind of selflessness is the ultimate tribute to your body and the best way to honor the ones you've lost.

The Weight of Butterflies

We are mirrors for each other, but we tend to mirror our own beliefs. We tell stories that reflect our distorted views. We make assumptions about life, based on the assumptions we make about ourselves.

For instance, we assume that life is as jealous and unforgiving as we are. When things go wrong, we assume life has judged us and found us guilty. We might have the view that disasters happen because we're sinful, or because a certain god is angry at us. Maybe a planet is in retrograde or the stars are out of line. Maybe life hates us, or nameless spirits want to punish us.

Rather than take responsibility for our actions, we prefer to feel victimized. Rather than recognize the truth, we tell different versions of the same stories. We attract those who agree with us. And, by mirroring each other's opinions, we create even more distortion.

We allow our own thoughts to drive us crazy. Our theories and ideas have the power to bring us down, as well as to lift us up. If we submit to the weight of our thoughts, we can easily feel crushed and defeated.

You don't think thoughts have weight? They don't; but they create the effect of a physical burden. Let me help you picture that effect. Imagine, for a moment the yearly migration of Monarch butterflies.

Every year, billions of butterflies travel thousands of miles to return to their birthplace. This happens on every continent on the planet. The Monarch is impressive. It's beautiful, and it has the strength to make the long journey home and back again.

Still, it's a butterfly. It's small, fragile, and as light as air. Butterflies are almost weightless, and yet, converged in numbers like these, they can cause the branches of massive trees to bend toward the forest floor.

A thought is far less substantial than a butterfly, but thoughts weigh heavily on us in much the same way. In physical terms, thoughts don't even exist. One thought may be too fleeting for us to notice, but obsessive thinking can cripple us.

Mental turmoil has the effect of crushing us. We slouch. Our shoulders droop. Our moods darken. Like mighty trees, our bodies visibly bend from the collective weight of our stories.

When we're emotionally vulnerable, our bitter thoughts can poison us. In a crisis, they can immobilize us. But we don't have to let them. At any time, we can turn them in a new direction. Or we can refuse to think.

Conscious non-thinking isn't child's play; it takes practice. With awareness, we can observe each flitting thought, the way we might watch one tiny butterfly in an open field. We can see it, appreciate it, and then let it drift away. This leaves our minds clear and at peace again.

Have you ever tried to be weightless, formless, while moving through the events of your life? Can you even imagine it? Without denying what's real, you can liberate yourself from mental noise and immerse yourself in the experience of life.

While most of us are collecting butterflies, life is happening everywhere. It has no thought and no opinion. Truth is hiding within every situation, and waiting to be discovered in any conversation.

It's not that hard to set yourself free from persistent opinions and old stories. Once you recognize the fragility of your thoughts, they won't seem heavy or intimidating. You'll find you can change them, or discard them. Thoughts are yours to manage. Beliefs are yours to choose.

Just as bones form the framework of your physical body, your beliefs support the framework of who you think you are. They shape the body of your reality. Within that body are virtual organisms—swarming thoughts and conversations that assume a life of their own.

You've spent years letting your thoughts create mischief. They trample through your brain like lawless kids, leaving muddy tracks everywhere. They create chaos and fear in your body, your home. And the same is happening to everyone.

Our thoughts drive us to distraction, or depression. Thoughts seem true, because they've been whispering to us since we first learned to think. They speak loudly, even when we say nothing. So we look for a diversion, or a means of sedation, and our lives suffer the consequences.

We humans are wrapped up in matter, yes, but we're also tangled up in our stories. Every thought tells a story. Every belief creates a mood. And, if we believe that death is terrifying, it will ultimately take the joy out of living.

With a conscious shift in your thinking, you can begin to reflect life in ways that inspire not only you, but the world you've worked so hard to create.

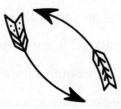

Day 3:
Grace

What is life? What is death?
How can we see what is, and is not,
when possessed as we are
by our little thoughts?

Good day again! Let's make sure our bodies are comfortable and our minds alert, as we investigate different perspectives of an important topic.

This week's discussion is about sparing ourselves unnecessary pain following a profound experience of loss. One such loss is the death of someone we love and feel we cannot live without.

As you recall, we approached this subject by first looking at life in its totality. We talked about energy and matter, and about life's creative process. Death is normal. The transformation of matter is inevitable.

Our existence is fleeting, yes; but while we exist, we can be aware of our own eternal and infinite nature. We can appreciate the nature of all living things and how each mirrors life differently.

Most of us focus on a much smaller perspective. We focus our attention on the events that make up an ordinary day. We worry over little frustrations and losses. We invest faith in a limited idea of ourselves. We ignore the big picture.

Today, we'll discuss how the mind can better reflect life, particularly in times of stress. The nervous system is a mirror for life. All creatures reflect life according to how they're made and how they perceive.

For human beings, life is reflected in story form. Energy is transposed into thought. We interrupt the flow of the plot with constant flashbacks, but our stories tend to move in a linear fashion. They have a past, a present, and a bunch of imagined futures. And they come with casts of players.

Everyone's story is filled with secondary characters. Some play bigger roles than others and some are incidental players. The most significant figure is the one who's telling the story. This is the main character, the person you imagine yourself to be.

Every story has its heroes, villains, and strong moral themes. What about yours? Do you see your life as a cautionary tale or an inspirational saga? Looking at it from one perspective, you may see it as a comedy. From another, it may seem like a tragedy. Maybe your life has an epic feel, littered with colorful characters and extraordinary circumstances. Then again, maybe the years of your life have gone by inconspicuously. You might have spent much of it on your own. You may see your own character as a victim, or perhaps as a hero to many.

Maybe your life has the quality of a one-man play, or a one-woman performance. However you see it, your life has provided a specific account of human history. You've been a legend in your time.

You tell your story when you're thinking. You tell it when you talk out loud. You describe the protagonist in different ways to different people. Now may be a good time to look more closely at that character and to make conscious choices about how it will drive you forward.

Now is the perfect time to notice how you respond to the events in your life. Are your reactions practiced or do they reflect this moment's reality? Do you follow the cues that society gives you or do you sense what is true and behave authentically?

It might be that you're still making choices based on your fear of losing things. It could be that you still react dramatically to everything. Death may be too horrifying for you to contemplate. Life may seem too whimsical.

Shadowy places need some light. Your fears need to be acknowledged. Your superstitions need to be confronted. Now is the time to look, listen, and nurture a better relationship with life... and death.

Paying Too Much

There's a story I like to tell about an alien girl from another planet who traveled to Earth. She was eager to see this planet and to understand the dream of humanity. First, however, she had to learn a few rules.

The first rule was never to pay more than ten cents for anything during her stay. The second was never to pay more than three times.

Pay no more than ten cents. Pay no more than three times.

If the rules are not followed, she was told, she would be trapped on Earth. She would be lost and unable to return to her own planet. So the girl vowed to remember, and embarked on her journey.

She arrived on Earth in the guise of a human being. Immediately, she found herself in the middle of a huge marketplace. All around her, merchants were selling their wares, shouting and waving to passing customers. People of all kinds were bargaining for the lowest price on clothes, food, and trinkets of every sort.

The alien girl took in the spectacle. Never had she witnessed such chaos. Everyone was yelling, and no one seemed to be listening. Everyone was competing to be heard and to be seen. In this marketplace, attention seemed to be the most valuable prize of all.

As she strolled through the stands, she caught the attention of a young man. He introduced himself, and took her hand. He treated her to cakes and candies. She found she enjoyed his company, and stayed by his side the rest of the day. The two of them laughed and played games for hours.

The girl experienced many things she never could have imagined and found pleasure in all of it. She found the young man to be especially amusing, so by the end of her day at the marketplace, she even felt she was falling in love.

As night came, the two friends danced by a beautiful lake and kissed in the moonlight. There were other dancers, too. There were many other girls, laughing and flirting, and before long, the young man was kissing someone else.

Much to her own surprise, the little alien felt surges of anger and jealousy. As the night wore on, these feelings became so strong that she could barely breathe. She could barely think. Confused and hurt, she ran away from the lake.

Soon, she was alone in a strange place at the darkest time of night. Gone was the marketplace and the colorful spectacle. Gone were the noisy crowds, where everyone talked and nobody listened. Gone, too, were the moonlight, the dancing, and the sweet comfort of a kiss.

Fear took hold of the girl. She ran and ran, going deeper into a dangerous landscape. She hardly saw where she was going. In her panic, she bruised her arms and legs on tree branches and cut her feet on hidden rocks. By dawn, she was lost and wounded.

For her brief adventure on this planet, she was paying a high emotional price. She was enraged. She was terrified. She was ashamed. On top of it all, she was hungry and cold.

When morning arrived, she limped into a small village where a kindly woman gave her some food and fresh spring water. While she ate, the girl listened to the woman talk about her own troubles.

It seemed the woman was alone, without a husband, and would soon be without a home. Recently, her only child had died of a fever, and she was filled with sorrow. She had lost everything that was precious to her.

The girl felt the woman's grief. As if the story had been her own. She felt the agony of losing a child. Soon, she began to cry. This moved the woman to cry as well. Together, they recalled their losses and fell into despair.

The poor woman would pay for her regrets, probably for the rest of her life. During the good times and the bad, she would relive her pain. She would blame herself for her misfortunes and her heart would break again. This was the way with all human beings, the girl realized.

Humans pay a thousand times for one mistake. They punish themselves, again and again. They spend their entire lives feeling regret for a single missed opportunity. They feel guilt, whether or not they are to blame.

And she, too, was punishing herself. She had been disappointed and driven mad with human jealousy. For a long time after, she would recall her first night on the planet and feel bitter again. Heartbreak would become a central theme in her life's story.

She would remember feeling betrayed. She would relive the horror of stumbling alone through the dark night. She would grieve for her friend, and for every woman who had lost a child. She would feel pity for all humans, and she would desperately yearn to be among her own kind.

Most of all, she would judge herself for breaking the two simple rules.

That's right. She had paid more than "ten cents." And she had paid it more than three times. She paid a high price for every disappointment, every loss. She paid again, every time she told her story.

And it seemed she would continue to pay. For the little alien girl would spend the rest of her life on planet Earth, remembering and regretting, just like every other person lost in the human dream.

How You Grieve

Grief is our emotional response to loss. It's our way of processing painful events; it's a way to heal. Grief demands that we rest and reassess.

Grief can also save us from our denials. If we allow it, grief helps us to see, to feel, and to measure our emotional strength. Having experienced the depths of our pain, we can welcome every possible change and move forward.

We can move forward, unless we choose not to. Grief can also be a prison sentence; it all depends on how we direct our attention. This is a choice. It can also be our salvation.

Without awareness, your attention will yield to old storylines. Reflexive thoughts will lead to emotional pain. You may judge yourself, and your judgments will then lead to more pain… and the cycle will continue.

We all let ourselves descend into darkness. Missing someone, we might visit a familiar hangout too often or play a favorite song until we're in tears. It's easy to let memories beat us up or let pain define us. We can stumble, even fall, but we need to get up and move again, sooner rather than later.

You do your best in every situation, and your best can mean anything from self-abuse to divine insight. You are a creature of Earth, but in many ways, you're unearthly. You are mortal and immortal, both. If you believe you're only the product of your thinking, thinking will remain your tyrant.

If you believe you're a victim, focusing only on your disappointments and dashed hopes, then you'll live as a victim. Feeling helpless, you'll want to strike out against someone. Striking out might make you feel guilty. Guilt will make you feel like a victim all over again.

Victimization, suffering, and then more victimization... the cycle may take years to stop, but you can begin to shake it off now. You can stop paying too much, too many times. You can make deliberate, constructive choices, if only for those who count on you to do your best.

The one you loved most, someone you didn't think you could live without, is gone. And here you are, having to live without them. You have to start another day, and then another after that, as a different kind of person.

Whatever the loss or the trauma, we all have to start again at some point. We have to reimagine ourselves and redefine our reality. This may seem hard, but we've been doing it all our lives. You've done it. You lost the thing that made life worth living, and you continued on. Or don't you remember?

First, you lost the safety and warmth of the womb. With physical birth, and the intrusion of light and air, you became another kind of being. It was a shock, but you adapted to life as a new human.

Later, you lost the sublime and uncorrupted state of infancy. You grew beyond that wordless knowing and began to learn things. You began to mimic the sounds and behaviors of everyone around you.

Words took over, and then judgments, and then a multitude of consequences for your actions. With your growing language skills, you bargained. You demanded. You acted out. You learned the game.

You probably don't realize how dramatically things changed since you first came into the world. Once, you were loved simply for being. And then, as you grew older, love might have seemed hard to find and even harder to keep.

You pushed on. You won love, you lost love, and you matured. You took the bad times with the good. You yielded to changes quickly. You experienced the thrills and the torments, knowing they were all part of life.

In adolescence, the rules changed again. Certainties became less certain. You thought things would stay the same, but they didn't. You thought you knew your body, but it became a stranger to you. You began to experience the fears and humiliations of near-adulthood. Nothing seemed as easy as it once did.

In your mind, you may still imagine yourself as the child, or the angry teenager, resenting the loss of carefree days and dreamless nights. Maybe you're the father or mother, longing for less complicated times.

You intuitively know what you have lost over the years, and yet you wake up each morning to face new challenges. You overcome fear. You survive losses of all kinds. You transform, over and over.

All of us have gone through the same experiences. We've lost things; but even by losing, we succeeded. We've stumbled; but even in stumbling, we moved closer to wisdom. We've reflected life's power to recreate and recover. We've been artists, always braced for a new perspective.

It's normal to grieve; but there comes a point when grief becomes the servant to our stories. The stories are usually about injustice or about missed opportunities. They're about our failures and shortcomings, or about some else's.

Maybe we think we had a role in the death of a loved one. Maybe we feel guilty for not making peace with the person we lost. "What do I do now?" we ask anxiously. "How can I go on?" We're worried about things we don't understand. "What happens after death? Where is my child now? Will we be together when I die?"

We torture ourselves wondering about the afterlife. We imagine that the dead are judging us. The stories we tell about death make us more afraid than we should be of death itself. These worries prolong our grieving and make a natural event unnaturally painful.

Fear cannot change what has happened. Being afraid doesn't honor the dead. Suffering isn't proof of loyalty. Grieving is not an excuse to harm the living.

We may say we don't want to destroy ourselves physically, and yet we seem willing to die, piece by piece, in little stages, from our own unchecked thoughts. In grief, the impulse to hurt ourselves might seem overwhelming.

Destruction may sometimes seem like the only course of action, and yet hurting ourselves goes against the true love of our lives: the physical body. It goes against the wishes of those we loved and lost. Above all, it goes against the will of life.

When you see yourself as someone who has lost a child, or a parent, death shocks and wounds you. You are its victim. When you expand your point of view, you may see everything differently. You are so much more than the roles you have played in your lifetime. You are the energy that makes this human life possible.

Death is matter; death is flesh and bone. You can see that you are the force that creates flesh and bone.

You are life itself; and life will take this body back someday, just as it has already taken someone you love.

Awakenings

Humanity has evolved. What humanity looks like today, even with its present problems, is not what it looked like five decades ago, and certainly not five centuries ago.

We humans also evolve as individuals. We arrive helpless and clueless, and yet we quickly learn to walk upright and communicate with the world. We learn to provide for our families. We learn to take advantage of our successes, as well as our failures.

We lose things and accumulate things. Most of our losses are small. We lose car keys and reading glasses. Sometimes we'll lose a wallet or a passport. We also know what it's like to lose a beloved home or a good job; but our losses can be even greater.

We sometimes lose a friend because of a careless word. We lose lovers and tightly-held dreams. We lose opportunities to be happy. We lose a sense of our own worth. We lose moments, memories, and the passions that once defined us.

As I've said, you and I know loss. We've known the still-ness of death and the startling sensations of rebirth. We've lost, but we've also won. We've cried and we've grieved, but we've also learned to laugh at adversity. We've modified our-selves so many times that we hardly notice the changes.

Losing a loved one feels like a thousand knives to the heart. And it will continue to feel that way until you make peace with the truth. You are life. Change is the essence of life, of energy and matter. Loss is nor-mal. To grieve is normal. To recover and to celebrate life again is also normal.

Humans have evolved to an impressive degree; so impressive that we might think we're better than all other forms of life on the planet. However, in basic ways, the life of a human isn't different from the life of any earthly creature.

We all eat, sleep, and create living copies of our-selves. Having eaten, we forage for the next meal. And then we rest. Sleep provides quality and vitality to our waking hours, so that we may continue to hunt for food and compete for a mate.

Without our biological appetites we can't continue as a species. It's the same for any animal, fish, or flower.

Some creatures sleep for months, perhaps years, in order to survive harsh winters or long droughts. Some change genders. Some change bodies. Survival is the point, it is the end game. Each species contributes in some way to the general well-being of others. Together, we contribute to the overall health of the planet.

Humans are complex, yes. We think and we imagine, but do we take full advantage of these talents? We can't seem to imagine our way out of our own stories. We're reluctant to challenge our core beliefs and opinions. We can't seem to quit old habits.

How many times do we end up apologizing for things we've said? How often do we regret something we've done, not just once, but repeatedly? And still, we'll probably find ourselves doing it again out of habit.

We can end a habit if we will it. We can change a point of view. We can see life as it is and not as we want it to be. "What's really happening right now?" we can ask ourselves, and be prepared to answer the question honestly. "What am I telling myself, and is any of it true?"

I'm inviting you to break a few rules when it comes to death and loss. I'm asking you to honor those you've lost in whatever way you find comforting, but be aware of beliefs that cause more pain. Don't participate in rituals that distress you. Don't continue traditions that make you fearful. Question them, or avoid them.

You've been in a walking, talking, sleep most of your life. The trauma of losing someone has disturbed that sleep, but it has also given you a chance to wake up fully. It has given you a chance to see, and to shake off illusion.

You have a chance now to trust life, whatever it brings.

The Hunt for Grace

All creatures hunt for food. We all need to eat to survive. Every species hunts in its own way, for its own kind of nourishment.

The mind isn't considered a species; but it, too, has an appetite. It has an appetite for emotions and will hunt for an emotional response in you and in other people. You could say that emotions make the mind feel real.

Taking this point a little farther, consider how your beliefs can inspire a certain kind of emotional appetite in you. If you believe that anger is your best defense in life, you'll find reasons to be angry about most things. You'll be sensitive to every small offense, and you will react with outrage.

If you believe your best efforts will always end in disappointment, you'll find ways to be crushed by failed expectations. You'll see failure as inevitable. You may even look for it, and develop an appetite for it.

Notice what you're thinking, and notice the emotional response that seems ready to follow. Your body has become so accustomed to your thoughts that it anticipates the usual cues. It's ready to respond with indignation, embarrassment, or guilt.

And, if you believe you're guilty, then guilt becomes your favorite food. You come up with ways that make guilt seem justifiable. "She makes me feel so guilty," isn't the truth, it's an excuse to eat what you crave.

No one "makes you" feel anything. You feel something because you think you should, or you must, and because you've created an appetite for it. You're hungry for self-pity or indignation. If the taste of shame is familiar and comfortable, you'll hunt it down.

We're all hunters, even those of us who don't appear to have an instinct for it. From the time we're born, we're searching for food. The food your body needs is very different from the food your mind demands.

Your body responds chemically to everything it perceives, and the result is an emotion. Emotions are real and always available, but we shouldn't be using them to hurt ourselves.

Emotions are real, yes. The stories that trigger our emotional responses are not real. We often claim to have no choice in the way we react to things, but we do. We have a choice. We have the ability to manage our reactions.

How addicted are you to fear, especially the fear of being judged? Be aware of how you hunt and why. Show accountability for your own emotional responses. See how you use a tragic loss to justify self-inflicted pain. See how it leads to other abuses.

How much do you crave the emotional energy of other people? Do you share their pain? Do you identify with their personal drama? Notice how you react to the misfortune of others. Maybe it feels good to be caught up in someone else's sorrow. You can acknowledge that and choose to hunt for a different food.

Truth enlivens us all. When you hunt authenticity, you're energized. You're happier, lighter. When your appetite shifts to the real and the true, your entire being can feel the difference.

Practice being honest with yourself, and lies will begin to leave a bad taste in your mouth. Any kind of drama will feel silly. Your emotional cravings will lessen. As you shake away old habits, you'll find that self-acceptance is the new habit. Trust in life is normal. Laughter is easy. Love is natural.

And, at last, you're willing to offer yourself a bit of grace.

Day 4:
Grace

How can a heart that is filled with fear
be a refuge for those who are here
and alive… who survived?

Greetings to you! It's good to have you here, awake and aware. Today, let's direct our attention to how we care for ourselves in times of grief and distress.

Life maintains an equilibrium and so must you. It's up to you to keep things in balance, whatever happens in the world around you. You are at the center of your world, a world that depends on you for its welfare and survival.

This planet of ours has survived a few cataclysmic events. Your body has, too. So have many of your beliefs. Old dreams get rearranged and some are extinguished and replaced by new ones. Meanwhile, your body, and the body of Earth, continue to spin.

Respect for yourself makes difficult situations less difficult. It's easier to survive a crisis when you love yourself. And the more aware you become, the stronger that love will be.

To be aware means to see life as it is. It means seeing other people as they are, without making judgments about them. It means seeing ourselves clearly. Although most of us claim to see things clearly, we make assumptions about almost everything.

Past events may not have happened the way we remember, but we swear we remember every detail. Future events can't be predicted, but we still try. We assume. We speculate. We expect. Rarely do we challenge what we think we know.

Losing someone has a devastating effect on both the body and the psyche. To avoid unnecessary pain, we need to be honest with ourselves. We need to put other people's opinions in perspective. We need to see more clearly.

We need to avoid the temptation to blame or to become hysterical. For many people, it isn't enough to grieve over someone's loss; every aspect of their lives must be touched by sorrow. Normal pleasures are spoiled by guilt and regret. Everyday activities like working, playing, or caring for children, become less enjoyable.

Some prefer to keep the pain alive for years. Misery, to some, feels like an act of love. Remorse feels like a duty. Suffering becomes an accepted tradition. We may be wise enough to know better, but we still feel we must suffer on behalf of those we lost.

For them, however, there is no suffering. For the dead, there is no worry, no struggle, and no fear. All the concerns of the world are over. So, to be honest, we grieve for ourselves.

"Oh, if I'd only done things differently," we hear ourselves say. "If I'd done more of this... or less of that." We pity ourselves, and expect to be pitied. We fail to see how all that suffering can affect the happiness of those around us.

Only you know if this is true for you. It may be that, in your grieving, you don't notice the pain you inflict on yourself. In your desire to be loyal to the dead, you might forget that your family needs balance and joy. And you need the same.

It's hard to imagine that your loved ones would want you to suffer. Your tribute to those who are gone is to make the best of the time that remains to you. Their lasting legacy is how you treasure memories of them.

Someone dear to you has died. The thing you feared most has happened. Now, fear shouldn't have such power over you. Now, you can find pleasure in small activities, and in the people who still look to you for love.

Now, you can trust life and feel its grace in everything you do.

The Many Deaths

Grace is a blessing, a gift that doesn't need to be earned. Life is the giver of grace. Reflecting life well, you can also be generous with love, even in the face of tragedy. Even in the middle of a crisis, you can be a safe refuge for others.

Every trauma presents a choice: to take productive actions, or actions that lead to your own defeat. The choice depends on how much love you give. Love yourself, and you can love others so much better.

The one you lost loved you too. Be respectful of yourself during times of stress. Give your heart the care it needs, even in your sorrow. Take care of your mind. Listen to your stories, and be willing to change.

Listen, without judgment. Notice where your thoughts are taking you, and shift their direction when you need to. How you think, and what you believe, can make a difference in your recovery.

The brain is designed to expect another moment to follow this one. It anticipates the near future, which means that it assumes there will be a near future. It's not built to anticipate its own death. It looks as far as the next morning or the next opportunity.

This makes it impossible for any of us to imagine the totality of death. And, even knowing that our time is limited, we still seem surprised when death hits close to home. Death is remote and something impossible to imagine when we're full of the energy of life. How else could we have moved through childhood with such abandon?

When we were young, we saw ourselves as invincible. Death was for the old and the ailing. When we were kids, we treated our bodies carelessly. We seemed to delight in dangerous things. Against all logic, we assumed we'd be the first to live forever. Youth doesn't smell the scent of death, although it permeates the air everywhere. Death is everything we see and touch.

Death is anything that breathes and moves. You, too, are made of dying stuff, along with the mysterious non-stuff that is the current of life.

Some traditions use phrases like "dust to dust" to describe a lifespan. But life forever returns to life. Dust is everything that happens in between. We're born, we kick up a whirlwind, and then fade into the haze as we move toward home.

This is the fate of every living thing. Eternity is home, and, on our way home, we lose some things. We lose people. Some of us, at some point, may have to watch our loved ones die.

No one can anticipate the aftermath of a tragic loss. You can't imagine the amount of strength you might have in the face of tragedy, nor can you predict your weaknesses. You don't know how you'll face the hurricane until it's upon you.

You lost someone. A dream has died, but you're still here. You're still aware and responsive to life. You can collapse under the weight your grief, or turn the power of grief into a creative force. Remember, you have a choice.

Permission to Laugh

Death is a thing that "cannot be named" for many people. In their minds, it's unlucky to talk about it. Most people don't want to talk about their own inevitable death and will only grudgingly talk about someone else's.

It's difficult to deal with tragedy when it happens to us. When it happens to someone close to us, we hardly know what to do. "What should I say? When should I say it?" More often than not, we say nothing, and let time do the work of softening our discomfort.

And, even without meaning to, we make judgments about someone's misfortune. Maybe he isn't as invincible as I thought, we might think privately. Maybe she's not as wise or as capable as she pretends to be. We see a flaw, or a weakness, and quickly make judgments.

Parents of dead children feel as though they've been marked for life. Surviving siblings sometimes feel the burden of having to live up to the legend of a dead brother or sister. How can any of us grieve in private when we're under such scrutiny?

Society makes grieving especially complicated. Whatever the event, we're expected to behave according to custom. Different social situations demand that we put on different faces. We're expected to mourn this way and to celebrate that way. If we do it our own way, judgments can be cruel.

Little kids often ask why they should change clothes for different occasions. Why wear pajamas at night, but a clean dress to school? Why not wear karate pants to a wedding, or scuba gear to bed? There's no good answer, except that changing clothes is what people do.

We all dress appropriately for important occasions, but we also want to set an appropriate emotional tone. A wedding and a funeral require different attitudes, although they both honor life. A church service is not a walk in the forest, although they can both be seen as a form of worship.

Changing moods, like changing faces, is a part of learning to be human according to the humans who raise us. Like so much of what we do, their rules helped us maneuver through childhood. But, again, we've grown up. Now, it's our responsibility to care for ourselves.

Now, it's our desire to be authentic. It's our job to be aware. We no longer need to follow public expectations. We shouldn't worry so much about what people think, or about pleasing our peers, our family, and our gods.

We want to be good enough, kind enough, and virtuous enough to meet society's standards; but then we blame ourselves for falling short of those standards. Instead, we can choose to feel whatever we feel.

Death doesn't discriminate. Events, good and bad, happen to everyone. Everyone suffers a loss at one time or another. Everyone feels pain and sorrow, and everyone will face death one day. Grief is meant to heal us, not add to sorrow.

Realities change for all of us. We change, too, despite our best efforts not to. Things change, our views change, but truth does not. Love does not. Love is a constant. And, like life itself, love imposes no conditions.

It's an act of love to acknowledge someone's strength and resilience in difficult times. It's an act of friendship to encourage laughter in difficult situations. A sense of humor gets us through unbearable moments. Good cheer should be viewed as a gesture of love.

Give yourself permission to laugh, to love, and to remember. Give others the same kind of tolerance. Give them the freedom to feel anything and everything. Be that kind. Be that generous.

Regardless of the circumstances, love yourself without conditions, and let the giddy wonder of that love spill out into the rest of the world like watercolors on a vast and expanding canvas.

Room to Feel

Grief is normal, yes, and also necessary. It takes us out of our present obligations and demands that we rest and reevaluate. It measures our emotional strength. Grief can help us to see and feel authentically. It can also make us more aware.

Then again, if we're not using our attention wisely, grief can be a lifelong burden. See how you grieve; notice how it affects your mood and your overall health. If you aren't paying attention, your thoughts will slip into old storylines. If you're not careful, you'll believe whatever stories you tell yourself.

Are you fully conscious? Are you aware of what you're thinking and saying, or just filling the silences? Are you being real with yourself, or satisfying other people's expectations? Are you awake? Are you really here?

Regardless of your pain, your body wants to maintain its connection with life. Make it your goal to feel more and to think less. Open your senses. Give yourself permission to see all sides to everything.

Let emotions come and go without judgement. Feel your fear. Feel guilt or shame without condemning yourself. Feel outrage without needing to act it out. Feel sorrow and also the strange intensity of your love. Grieve, and know that grief doesn't define you.

Feeling everything means permitting yourself to experience a bad day or a heart-wrenching night, and to find your way through the pain. It means finally being at peace with the truth. If you're afraid to feel you might also be afraid to live.

Sometimes different things want to be felt at once. Can you really feel sorrow and wonder, simultaneously? You can. Is it possible to be filled with rage and also with a gentle appreciation of life? It is. Can joy, torment, and a sense of calm coexist in you? They can, and they will.

Boundless love can sit with resentment and despair. Comprehension may trickle through blinding confusion. You can hurt and still laugh. You may feel grief's heavy weight even while you seem to float above it.

Every emotion needs to be acknowledged and expressed without making anyone the target. It doesn't matter if you're furious, defeated, or resigned. It doesn't matter if you hate. However scary or unpleasant, every feeling counts.

Once fully expressed, an emotion won't haunt you as it did before. You're not so vulnerable to your own stories. You're not so easily seduced by habits that were born out of fear.

Humans feel. You and I can't risk not feeling. Your body produces emotions; it does this for your health and survival. Get used to the idea of feeling everything without having to act any of it out.

What does "acting out" mean? We're acting out when we try to pull someone else into our drama. We're acting out when we subject other people to our emotional tirades. Remember that your grievances are yours to resolve, not theirs.

Acting out isn't about mourning a loss, it's usually about getting attention. Maybe your appetite for drama ended long ago. Good. Maybe you no longer rage against life's injustices. Even better. You may have already realized that complaining drives people away and that you'd rather stay close to the people you love. This is the reward for waking up and becoming aware.

Even if you haven't fully learned these lessons, you can learn now. You can learn to replace selfish habits with generous ones. You can practice sitting quietly with yourself, and to be as honest as you know how to be. You can learn to enjoy the taste of truth.

I mentioned before that, with self-awareness, your lies will leave a bad taste in your mouth. Your self-deceptions will start to feel uncomfortable. They may become intolerable. Truth will become your favorite food.

Truth is life, not your theories about life. Truth is what you feel and touch, not any opinions about what you feel and touch. Truth is you, not the knowledge you think defines you.

Try this, until it becomes automatic: think of nothing, hear nothing, and then take stock of what you're feeling. Chances are you can't put a name to many of your emotions. Why should you? Name one and knowledge takes over. So, just feel. Feel and relax.

Notice small agitations and allow your body to feel safe again. Say it out loud, in fact. "I'm safe. There's no danger here. Not now, not ever." When your breath is slow and deep again, begin to feel what's going on around you.

What's happening with the people close to you? Feel the people you love, who are surviving loss as well as they can. Feel, from their point of view. After that, you can open your senses even more, and feel the emotions of people you don't know. That's right, billions of people are feeling every possible response to every kind of event. They, like you, are paying an emotional price for each of their stories. Feel the ongoing heartbreak. Feel the irrepressible delight. Feel the collision of passions that amounts to the human experience. Feel the frenzy of this collective dream, rippling along the calm surfaces of Earth.

Feel the emotional tornado, even while you sit quietly at its center. Feel death, loss, and renewal. Feel the desperate urge to live. Feel love, binding each of us to someone else. Feel joy, rage, and serenity merge and become the full force of life.

Feel that force. From now on, let it inform you. Release your attachment to what you think you know. Defend your opinions less. See everything from life's point of view.

From life's point of view, there's no right or wrong. There's no good or bad. There's no loss and no gain. And from life's point of view, there's nothing to forgive.

Forgiveness

For thousands of years, humans have understood the wisdom of forgiveness. We've known that it frees us from the heavy restraints we put on our hearts. We've known that the penalty for not forgiving is to suffer even more.

And yet, forgiveness is a kind of magic that we're reluctant to practice. Blaming seems more righteous. Anger seems more logical. Suffering feels more like justice. Once again, the price we pay is too high, and we're willing to pay it much too often.

No one is ever really prepared for trauma or its aftermath. We're barely able to keep up with the disturbances that occur in an ordinary day. We're vulnerable to the judgments we make against ourselves. We're defenseless against our memories.

Few of us were taught to love ourselves, no matter what. Fewer were really shown the healing power of forgiveness. But, in the end, our greatest healing comes from forgiving ourselves.

I can almost hear you ask, "Forgive myself for what?" Well, you might want to forgive yourself for whatever role you think you played in a tragic event. You might forgive yourself for keeping old injuries alive, at your own expense, or for allowing anger and bitterness to corrupt your natural impulse to love.

You can forgive yourself, because you did not know. You can forgive others for the same reason. They, too, live their own dream and can't see the effect they have on other lives. Few of us know what our actions will do to affect future moments.

Forgiving allows you to redirect your energies to other people and other passions. It unburdens you from the weight of a tragic story. It gives you a rest from ongoing grievances, if only long enough to see yourself through the eyes of love.

You may feel uncomfortable to turn your affections inward. You might not know how to pause, take a breath, and deliver a message of tenderness to your body. It probably feels awkward to give yourself a hug, but it's a habit worth getting used to.

Your mind, by resisting the idea of death, may actually help you. In moments of trauma, the mind is shocked into silence. As the shock wears off, all the stories begin again. So, take advantage of the silences and feel. Find your connection with life, and allow forgiveness to heal your deepest emotional wounds.

In the months and years following someone's death, it may seem like you're floating on a depthless ocean of sorrow. It may seem impossible to stay above water. You may be paddling, attending to your daily routines, and a wave will rise to overwhelm you. Or an undertow will pull you down. This, too, is normal.

Regardless of your efforts to stay afloat, the sorrow sometimes wins. There's no shame in allowing yourself to feel the pain fully rather than denying it. Submerge yourself in feeling, without thinking. Breathe in your sorrow. Breathe in the fear and the hurt. Avoid none of it.

In a small space of time, the truth can become more visible to you. It can even feel undeniable. You may feel closer to life. Your body can feel its generosity, even in the deepest point of despair.

When you come back to the surface, breathe in new joy. Breath in gratitude and forgiveness. Feel your loved ones in the air, in the sunlight, and in every living thing. Remember that your mind can be as flexible as life is. It can be adaptable to change. It can console the body with kind words or blessed silence.

When death leaves you bereft and confused, your mind can be a loyal friend. Don't be afraid to show the world what that friendship looks like. Float, swim, or fly—do one, do another, or do them all. Take your time to feel, and trust life to support you.

Existence is meant to instruct us. Death is a necessary part of the teaching. The mind should learn these important lessons and not obstruct them. Grief should be allowed to take us to new levels of wisdom while we still live.

Accepting Normal

Everyone wonders how they would face the unthinkable. Would they handle a tragic event differently? Would they be better at it, or worse? Would they be brave or would they fall apart at the mention of a lost friend or family member? Would they give up and hope to die?

It's important to keep asking the question. "How do I feel?" The answer is always changing, just as we are changing and learning. Losing someone has a devastating effect on both the body and psyche. What we feel is likely to be beyond words and beyond tears. We need to be as honest with ourselves as possible.

You may be saying, "Sorry, it's too late for that. My regrets are too many to count, too profound to express. My sorrow is too painful to bear. My memories are already torturing me, and every thought leads me to anger and shame."

We all get caught up in daily routines and forget to check on ourselves. Our attention swings erratically, from family, to jobs, to social ambitions, to romantic liaisons. Things happen. Some choices we make hurt the people we care about the most.

Only after losing someone do we see the opportunities to do it all better. We see how we sometimes exceed our own expectations and also how we fail them. We're the hero, as well as the villain, of our own story.

We're attentive parents and we're also absent when our kids need us. We're good friends and, very often, neglectful ones. We're generous lovers but we're occasionally selfish and temperamental. We're great at life… when we aren't awful at it. This is normal.

Here you are, now, faced with more choices. Do you give up or step up? Do you grow dimmer or shine brighter? Does your fear get stronger or does it fade in the brilliance of your own light?

Emotional pain is normal. So, too, is the fear that your pain will never subside. The pain you feel won't go away completely. It has already become a part of you. That's normal, too.

In the course of creation, death is normal. So is loss. So are the consequences of what we do in the wake of loss. It's normal to grieve and it's normal to learn from our grieving and recover from it.

Just for a second, acknowledge your pain without making excuses for it. Free your mind of all its judgments. Reject thoughts that poison you. Imagine your own sorrow losing its weight and density, until it's able to float away on a cheerful wind. You're the one who imagines and makes an idea come to life. You're the one making choices at every moment. Only you can soothe your bruised heart. You may choose not to. You may believe it's appropriate to suffer in the wake of a tragedy. You might even believe you don't deserve to be happy, or that you don't deserve to be alive.

"I can't go on," you may be thinking. In a way, it's true. You can't go on as you were. Loss has forever changed you. This is how it's been throughout your life. This has always been your genius: finding more ways to be you.

Throughout your life, you've worn various faces for various situations. You've changed outfits and attitudes to fit every occasion. Now you may choose another way to be. Now you may suspect that, under all the masks you wear, there's an authentic human being waiting to be discovered.

Where Do I Go From Here?

Losing a loved one is devastating and there's no way to soften its impact. You may feel the repercussions of it for a very long time. You may pity yourself and willingly accept the pity of others. Or, you may decide to honor life by investing your energies differently.

Emotions need to flow freely through you. In a healthy environment, they touch you, instruct you, and change you. There's no safety in holding on to a feeling and refusing to let it go.

Your mind can do a lot to alter its own narrative. It can act as a friend during the healing process or it can be your worst enemy. Instead of letting your thoughts dictate how you feel, turn them into allies. Rely on them to protect you and support your desire to love.

Because you believed something once doesn't mean you should still believe it, or that it was ever true. Remember the little child who believed in fairy tales, and take comfort in the fact that you've grown up.

Respect everyone's right to have a point of view; but no one has the right to impose beliefs on you. Be skeptical of what they say, but listen. Decide for yourself what is true, keeping your health and well-being in mind.

Everyone has opinions and they aren't always shy about sharing them. People are happy to give sympathy and advice. They're quick to offer a quote from somewhere, a profound phrase, or a proverb.

People say many things, intending to help. They say that time heals. They say that life's unfair. They say that there's nothing worse than death and that only the good die young. They say that we're not supposed to outlive our children, but some of us do. Well-meaning friends can sometimes make us feel worse than we already do. "This is the worst thing that can happen," they might say. "How awful for you! You must feel so guilty!"

They may whisper things like, "He'll never get over this!" They may insist, "She doesn't deserve this!" Some people will pity you. And you may feel tempted to pity yourself. Some will avoid you.

People may support your worst stories. They may encourage your deepest fears. Good intentions may do nothing to ease your pain... and superstitions can make things much, much worse.

Hoping to find some light in the darkness, you might decide to explore new religions. You might turn to ancient myths. Maybe you'll talk to a psychic or a fortune teller. In your grief and fear, you might be tempted to entertain the irrational. It's not unusual for people to call on ghosts and spirits for comfort. They want to imagine a loved one being in "a better place," or keeping company with angels. For some, it helps to imagine that the dead continue to watch over us, that they've returned as beautiful creatures flying above the human dream.

It's nice to think someone has come back as the hawk that just swept past the kitchen window or the stray dog that ambled up to the house. We want to see our beloved in the first blossom of spring or as a dove wooing its mate.

We want to recognize something of them in the grace of a deer or the eyes of a coyote. If the people that we've lost can live so vividly in our imagination, they must still exist as something else, somewhere else.

Is there an afterlife... is there a heaven, or a hell? Can I speak to the dead? Is my loved one watching over me? Listen carefully to how you, the survivor, cope with death. See how you pitch one idea against another, urging your mind into a battle with itself.

We're all tempted to glorify the dead. We want to imagine them as saints, and to picture them sitting close to God. We'd love to see them running through sunlit fields. We want to hear them, see them, and be reassured by them.

Death, however, doesn't become more understandable through stories. Superstition has the power to govern us. It has the power to hurt and confound us. It has power because we give it power; but without the benefit of our faith, superstitions have no power at all.

Energy is power. Matter is real. What is more astonishing than flesh and bone being wrapped around the incomprehensible truth? What story can match the full intensity of this moment?

What theory is more astonishing than the spark of a neuron or the loping pulse of your heart? What is more awe-inspiring than your own evolution? Nothing. Nothing is more amazing than the truth of you.

You've evolved in so many ways. A fetus became a bouncing baby and then an engaging child. More physical transformations propelled you into adulthood. You've become so accustomed to these dynamic changes that your mind can't imagine an end to it. What is the next phase? it wants to know. What will I be after this? Where do I go from here?

It's the mind's job to know things, but it cannot know death. Why do we live and then stop living? There's no real answer to this, but mankind has made up a million stories in its effort to find answers.

Recite the words of poets and prophets if that eases your pain. Appeal to guardian angels or spirit guides. Believe in something that resonates as true, for your own healing. Believe it, fortify yourself, and then let it go.

You are not your stories and superstitions. You are life in its entirety, looking at yourself through the smallest possible lens. Wise men and women don't fear death; they recognize themselves as the one, infinite and eternal force. There's no reason you can't be just as wise and just as aware.

Tell yourself the stories that give you comfort. Then, tell your child's story. Tell your lover's story and your mother's and your father's story. Tell your story. It's the most teachable mythology of all.

Tell the story of how your life was changed by the person you loved and recently lost. Describe how your life will continue without their presence. Honor the lives of the people you value by living yours to the fullest.

Remember the lover that you miss and the intimacy that you shared. Remember, and be comforted. Remember your sweet child, always eager to cuddle. Remember your parent, or friend, and marvel at their constant support of you.

Remember what this wonderful human being meant to your life. Remember the face, the voice, and the touch of a hand. Remember and be thankful, but also know that the people you loved were never just men, or women, or precious babies. They were life. They were life, just you are now.

In your eagerness to believe in something, remember that you are life itself. Smoky Mirror, our medicine man in the desert, had that revelation. He saw that his body was made of stars and the space between the stars. And he knew this was true of everyone.

Everyone is made energy merged with matter. No other story is as compelling as that. You don't need to imagine the face of a loved one in a cloud. You are the cloud. You are the morning star and the midnight moon. And, yes, you are the coyote, the hawk, and the howling wind. Whatever life is, you are.

You are the light that sparkles in a child's eyes and in the smile of a stranger. You are the smallest breath and the greatest achievement. You are everything, everywhere, even while you live.

Day 5:
The
Elegy

I am the force that creates and,
for everything born,
obliterates.

Hi, again! We've come to the final day of our conversation on death and loss, and I'd like to begin it with another story.

First, let's admit that stories are a human art, but that we humans don't always approach our storytelling as artists. Clearly, our thoughts needle us. We even seem willing to let thoughts defeat us. We let our mental chatter go unnoticed until it sickens our bodies and brings ruin to our dreams. Knowing this, we can change it.

Language is a sacred art. Words give us the opportunity to communicate with all of humanity, not just ourselves. The art of storytelling is meant to lift us up, as individuals and as a species.

So, just like our best legends, even casual thought can teach us how to be wiser. Every quiet idea can mirror the truth. Even during a crisis, our minds can produce memory-stories that offer stability and comfort.

There's a comforting tale that I heard once as a child about a kind man whose wife passed away at a young age. His love for her was so strong that he swore he could never be happy without her. So he continued to grieve, for years and years.

He began each day feeling heavy sorrow. He prayed each night that God would take him soon, so he could be with his beloved wife again. He found it difficult to be around people, so he avoided family and friends.

Every day, he would visit his wife's grave, crying out in grief. One such day, as the man sobbed over her grave, he became aware of an odd noise. It sounded like someone was strumming a guitar and singing.

Singing, in a cemetery? Impossible! This upset the poor man so much, that he stood up and stalked angrily toward the music.

Not far from where his wife was buried, he found a young man sitting on a gravestone, playing a guitar. He looked completely at peace, cherishing each note he played, and smiling to himself as he sang:

"With a song and a smile, I'll linger a while,
And follow the will of—"

"What are you doing?" the man interrupted. "Don't you know where you are?"

The singer stopped playing and looked up with a smile. "Yes, sir," the younger man answered pleasantly. "I'm at the grave of my beautiful wife, the woman I loved more than anything in the world."

"Your wife is dead?" the older man responded. "And you smile? You sing?"

"Yes. She is gone, and I must face the world without her." He lifted his guitar in the air. "I must follow life's will, as must we all."

"By singing?" the grieving man choked.

"Singing, yes! And dancing. And then singing some more!" said the other man, as he took up his guitar and continued his verse.

"Here am I, alone and bereft,
having lost my love, my friend, and my wife!
What can we do, when there's nothing left,
but follow the will of life?"

The young man's voice was clear and his eyes were bright with love. As he sang, he rose to his feet and stepped cheerfully around the nearby graves.

"With a light heart and a smile,
I'll dance for a while,
And follow the will…follow the will…
follow the will of life!"

This story is like many others told throughout history. It teaches us to honor and respect life, whatever occurs. It urges us to appreciate life's generosity, even in the face of loss. Rather than encouraging us to see every unpleasant event as an injustice, it gives us another point of view.

The will of life seems simple: we creatures are born into existence. We live, we create more life, and then our physical bodies die. There is no natural law that says any living thing should survive this long or that long, or that we should live one way or another.

Grief is an authentic response to losing someone. It's a song we humans sing to the dead, young and old, but its melody is familiar to many other species. The experience is shared by countless living beings.

Grief is also an elegy, a poem, written into our genetic fabric. The theme of an elegy is love: love for what was, love for what is, and for what may still be possible. You could say that grief is our tribute to all that is destroyed in the process of creating more life.

To grieve is normal, but allowing grief to defeat joy is not. To rage at the passing of a loved one is normal, but keeping the rage alive is not. Missing the love of a child, or a spouse, is normal, but using love as an excuse to hurt ourselves is not. When happiness isn't given the fuel it needs, we remain inconsolable.

Death gives us the chance to rejoice at having known someone. It also tempts us to feel guilty, as we regret what was never said and never shared. It gives us the incentive to bond, but also to blame.

This choice belongs to each of us, as artists.

The Artist

Grieving is one more expression of humanity's art. The choices we make in the aftermath of loss are creative choices. How we respond to death affects our appreciation for beauty and our enthusiasm for the days ahead.

Of course, no one can choose whether or not to feel pain. It hurts to lose someone. The question is whether to let the pain consume us. Will it destroy everything we've created? Will grief take us down a path of destruction or will it inspire us to create?

Whatever you decide, the pain has already become a part of you. It's now set into the mosaic that is your life. It has changed the shape of your world and composed a different melody to move you through it.

To continue to love generously and without conditions, even while mourning the death of a loved one, is artistic excellence. To accept what is given, as well as what is taken away, is to obey the will of life.

An event has changed you. How you live out your years is a matter of will. You can't make authentic choices when you're bound to the roles you play. Your will is not your own as long as other people's opinions determine your actions.

Free will, you could say, is the privilege of the artist. It's carried out at the discretion of the artist, who may submit to public pressure or make revolutionary choices for the sake of art.

An artist may choose one style, or many. So may you. You can be innovative and experimental. You can celebrate your art or undervalue it. You can create lasting beauty or destroy a work of art before it's fully appreciated.

Imagine a painter, excitedly brushing colors onto a canvas. He might paint for hours, and then, in an instant, decide to paint over it all and start something new. This is an act of free will. This is the process of creation.

Imagine a potter, molding something out of clay. She may set out to make a bowl, and in a flash of mad inspiration, rework the clay into a delicate statue. In the act of creating one thing, something else is lost.

Smoky Mirror, our shaman in the desert, was an artist, too. He was willing to question his own vision of reality. He was willing to push past acceptable beliefs and teachings, to embody the truth. Every culture evolves through the vision and courage of its artists.

In Buddhist and Hindu cultures, creating a masterpiece called the mandala is a meditative practice intended to connect the inner and outer worlds. Mandalas are works of art, painted or constructed out of colorful objects. They are most often geometric patterns built using sand, grain by grain, with special care given to color, design, and symbolic meaning.

After days or weeks of creating an intricate design out of sand, the work is destroyed. The sand is brushed into a pile and spilled into running water to spread its blessings.

A human life is a work of art. It takes countless days of evolution to bring an infant safely into adulthood. It takes a million moments of happiness and hardship to create a friend, a child, or a sweetheart.

Destroying it may only take a second. It may take just one action or a thoughtless choice. Still, that creation changed everything, and its intricate beauty remains a source of inspiration to those who survived.

We live as humans for a brief time. We exist as meditations on truth and testaments to the wonder of life. Every living thing is a mandala, providing us a sense of peace and reminding us of the certainty death.

You and I are intricate works of art that are not meant to last. Your life, too, is made more rewarding and complex by the people you knew and lost. You don't have to think about art, you feel it. You experience it in a mysterious way any time you bring it to mind.

Those who have died still live on in our minds. Their stories teach us. Their faces and their bodies inspire us to love. Remembering them should bring us peace, not sorrow. Visualizing someone's smile, or a gesture, should move us beyond our grieving.

One single life can dazzle us. It can influence many. It can change worlds or light up a tiny corner, but the light goes out eventually. Its colors fade. Its patterns blur and run.

Eventually, the masterpiece is swept up, and its blessings spill into the current of human memory.

Art and The Will

Living is an art. So in that sense, we are all artists. The people we lost were also artists. They contributed to their time in history. They were shaped by global events and personal circumstances. Their beliefs and desires produced a once-in-forever dream.

Art is made to please and to provoke. Art moves us and engages us. Art captivates and inspires us, but art is not made to last. However worn and damaged we think we are, each of us is a piece of art in human form. And that form, too, isn't meant to last.

We build our palaces, knowing someday they will be reduced to ruins—fleeting testaments to our genius. We create something of beauty and then send that little masterpiece off to meet its fate. Sooner or later, it will be lost to history.

Still, we're all sensitive to loss. Priceless artifacts are stolen and historic structures are destroyed in the ugliness of war. We mourn their destruction. We mourn the loss of mankind's reason and goodwill. We fear for mankind itself.

And we celebrate recovery, like finding sunken treasures or ancient scrolls. We search for signs of forgotten civilizations. We collect things. We cling to each other. We value rare objects as we value human life.

Ask yourself how it feels to create something. It feels right. It feels wonderful. If you raised a child, cultivated a close friendship, or built a business, do you regret having done any of it? Do you wish you'd never invested the effort?

You were also creating a personal history. If you think you failed at any part of it, you're missing the point of existence. This magnificent "failure" is your art. Everyone's creative process is messy and exhausting, but it results in something that will never be seen or experienced again.

Picture soap bubbles floating in a breeze. Notice how sunlight adorns each one with unique patterns of swirling colors. Soap bubbles are delicate, fleeting things. With a puff of air, they're born. They dance and spin. Then, with a pop they're gone. Whatever traces they've left evaporate quickly in the heat of the day.

Creating something beautiful is worth the effort, even if it gives you only the briefest pleasure. Your life is an ongoing creative effort. Your life is your art, and death is part of its wonder.

You create art with an eye for beauty. An evolving point of view is natural to your creative process. Why not look at death like that?

Your own death will be a unique expression of your art. The death of a loved one should be seen the same way. Respect their talents. Don't judge them through the lens of your disappointments. Whether they died very young or very old, value their art.

Give your full respect to the artists you lost. And give yourself that small bit of grace as you move forward without them.

It doesn't matter whether you think of yourself as wise or unworldly. It doesn't matter if you speak easily or find it difficult to speak at all. Your art reaches far beyond words and your artistic talent continues to evolve.

You are the central character in a dream of your own making. Your life is a distinct work of art, shaped by your own ways of thinking and imagining. You've built a reality out of all the things you learned. And you're still building. Like life itself, you're building, unbuilding, rebuilding, and reinventing.

Life, the supreme artist, creates and destroys at the same time. Change comes with upheaval and sometimes death. Trees sprout new growth from the rich legacy of decaying leaves. With old roots, we plant ourselves into the soil of a new dream, welcoming new friendships and new opportunities.

You, the artist, have faced these same changes throughout your life. You've transformed as you've grown. Your body's cells have replaced themselves many times over the decades. Your mind has replaced one belief for another. Old images of yourself have been discarded for new ones. Habits have ended and passions forgotten.

Maybe you've had to move from town to town in your lifetime. Along the way, you've discarded precious items, emptied rooms, and driven away from familiar realities. Simultaneously, you've created new realities in other places. You've furnished other houses and painted other walls.

You've watched young gardens grow and left others to perish. You've torn down, rebuilt, and kept moving forward. You've created new realties from the remnants of old ones. And now you have the chance to do that again.

Great artists rebel against social expectations. Surrendering to life's inspirations, they will ignore their critics. Following their own creative will, they may even break the rules that brought them to greatness.

Artists exercise free will. You are the artist of your personal reality, improving your skill with every revelation. You are your own masterpiece, modifying yourself with every new experience. You are the student, teacher, and the sum of all you've learned. You're also the product of all human experience. You know what victory feels like, and also despair.

Every human experience lives within your genetic memory. You may not be a father who lost his only child, but that experience is part of you. You know what is to be a boy who lost a brother or a lonely girl who lost a friend. You are a child, raised without a mother, and you are a grieving widow, inconsolable and alone.

You are the human experience, complete with its cruelties and immense joys. Every human experience is filled with small joys and astonishing delights. Death is balanced by the breathtaking excitement of birth. Every loss is balanced by countless gains.

No disappointment should be ignored, no joy forgotten. Pleasant memories, as well as unpleasant memories, have made your life the poetic composition it is. And when memory has lost its power over you, love is what remains.

Memory Games

Death, birth, and rites of passage are events. So are all the little moments in your life that pass unnoticed. In fact, you are an ongoing event. Your life began at a certain point, evolved, and will continue to evolve until the event of your death.

Your relationships, too, are events; and human relationships work better when you remember to treat yourself kindly, especially under stress. Any situation improves when you respect the people close to you, especially in times of grief.

Every event teaches you something. Your response to any situation tells you something about yourself. A thought, or an image, is a virtual event that triggers real emotions. So are your preoccupations with the past.

Since you're good at imagining things, picture a family of ducks skimming on the surface of a river. It's a happy picture. Observe them as they speed along with the current for a while, occasionally dipping their beaks into the water and enjoying the scenery.

The river rushes them along, but they won't travel too far downstream. At some point, ducks turn around. They defy the current. They flap their wings and fly back to where they started.

That's how they spend their day. Ducks float downstream, fly back upstream, and start all over again, repeating the same ride over and over like kids at a waterpark.

We can't do that. We can't replay our lives, but that doesn't mean we don't try. We can't resist flapping our mental wings, hoping to propel ourselves out of the present to some other place. Only later do we realize that we've lost the moment and missed the scenery.

The past has already been lived. There's no experiencing it again. We can't duplicate the wonderful moments and we dare not repeat the painful ones. There's no comfort in reconstructed memories. There's nothing to gain from guilt and regret.

"I could have stayed with her that night," we might say of a deceased parent. "I didn't have to shut him out," we might say of a friend. We wish we hadn't done that, or said that, or implied that. We wish we could do it all over.

The mind is a historian, a commentator. It documents what's going on, minute by minute. It makes judgments about what's right, wrong, safe, or dangerous. Most of the stories it tells are borrowed from other imaginations, but it's been faithful to those stories since childhood.

Our mental narratives go on and on like a favorite audio book. We've heard every bit of the dialogue before, but we keep listening. We know the plot, but still seem surprised by it. We get the message, but we can't move on.

We've come to believe what we think; what we think, our bodies feel. Think of something that made you angry in the past, and you'll feel that anger again. Think of a betrayal, a disappointment, or a loss, and you'll feel miserable again. It doesn't matter how many years have passed since then.

Every time you recall a disturbing event, your body will produce feelings of fear or dismay. It doesn't take a death in the family to bring you down. Watch yourself in ordinary moments. Watch how preoccupied you are by painful memories.

"Hey! Where did you go?" People ask when they've lost your attention. You're there, but not there. You're choosing to focus on a memory instead of them. You're engaged in an imaginary conversation. You're sitting in one place, while your mind's in another.

We can't make the past better, but we can surely make the present worse. Why would we want to? *Now* is an uncorrupted moment, since it hasn't yet committed to a story. *Now* is free of worry and ripe for imagination. *Now* can play with infinite possibilities; the past cannot.

What you once had, you no longer have. What was, no longer is. There is no answer to, "Why did such a lovely person have to die?" She did die. He did die. There's no arguing with life. There's no negotiating with the truth.

Mortality is one of life's countless gifts to us. Acknowledge the wonder of it. Express real gratitude for all that has happened and is about to happen. Remember that change almost always comes with disturbance.

Change and disturbance; these are not bad words. They describe life. They describe your life, then and now. Someone you know has died. You can't go back to the way things were. You have to make things okay, right now.

You may have asked yourself many times what it means to "live in the moment," and the simple answer is to pay attention to what's going on right now.

Feel an event, see it as it is, and respond to it authentically.

Authenticity is something you lost touch with way back at the start of your life's journey. You spent your early years practicing the right responses. You learned the game of pleasing people and soon became a master at it.

It might seem risky to undo all that work, and your efforts may have unpredictable consequences. What will happen if you stop bending to expectations? How much will you lose? How will people see you then? Who will you be?

Reclaiming authenticity takes time and practice—the sort of practice it took to lose it so long ago—and uncertainty isn't an excuse to stop growing. You want to feel safe, yes, but there's not much safety in the old and familiar. There's no refuge in lying, however much it seemed to have protected you in the past. The only safe-haven is now.

Now can offer you something you've never experienced before. On the other side of now is awareness. Awareness is about finding comfort in this moment, whatever the moment offers.

In the moment you're experiencing, make the choice to be authentic. Take a spontaneous action and notice its impact. Say something honest and feel its resonance. Develop a taste for the truth.

Authenticity is irresistible. Truth is attractive. Who isn't attracted to an honest and clear-sighted person, even if they're judged to be eccentric? People sometimes react uncomfortably to authentic behavior. They may see it as naive, but it also inspires their respect.

Say no when you mean no. Say yes when you mean yes. Say nothing if your opinion is unwelcome. Silence is allowed. Listening is recommended. Listen to what you're thinking. Don't believe it, but learn something from it.

Admit what you're feeling, even if it seems unpleasant. You may feel intense rage or the anguish of injustice. You may feel shame that you escaped death when someone else did not. You may feel a gaping emptiness inside, knowing that you will never again share moments with a person you loved beyond words.

Living in the moment means using all the personal power available to you. Only in this moment do you have the power to shift your point of view. Right now, you have the power to conquer your fears and make peace with death. Now, can you make the choice to love yourself and to enjoy every moment life affords you.

You don't have to run from what is, or from what was. You don't need to run from what will be or may never be. You can welcome any possibility. You can get along with now, even in hard times.

The only reality is now, and right now is gone in the blink of an eye. It turns into another moment, and then another. It turns into another realm of possibilities for healing, forgiving, and sharing love.

Each present moment delivers infinite possibility. It connects you to pure energy and pure power. This moment will affect all future moments, as it will affect your memories of the past.

While you're agonizing over a memory, hesitate and give thanks. Be grateful for the many sweet experiences that life has provided, as well as the painful ones. Turn your grief into a conscious act of creativity. Do something. Make something.

Compose a piece of music. Draw a picture. Describe your pain, in words, lyrics, or poetry. Don't shrink from the truth. This now will be followed by another, and then another.

Countless nows will make a day, a month, and all the years of creativity that lie ahead.

Life's Music

Your beliefs and opinions are not the truth of you. You're not just the conversation running in your head, you are the moment. You are life, filled with potential.

You've been posing as the central character in your own story. You've put your faith in the familiar traits and memories of that character. You've defended those traits and you've judged yourself according to those memories. You're reluctant to go against what people expect of that character.

How you define yourself is as much a result of other people's opinions as it is the product of your judgments about yourself. Having come so far in your awareness, you can now consider giving that character up.

Just as you form a thought or align yourself to any idea you can also stop believing that you exist apart from life. Unite your mind to the creative power of life, like you would perform a wedding ceremony.

Merging with life is not a challenge, since life is what you are and have always been. The challenge is to let go of all the stories, all the rambling thoughts, that make you feel separate from life.

Until now, your knowledge has served the desires of an imaginary character. Instead, let your knowledge serve the will of life. Give your words the power to enlighten, not diminish, you. As you would lay down any weapon, discard your doubts and fears. Let judgments end and put your faith in the truth of you.

Move to the soothing melodies of nature. We all feel energized by a walk in the mountains or a day by the ocean. We relax in the company of a pet. We enjoy listening to the sounds of songbirds. In other words, we naturally follow nature's music, but we can also do it consciously.

In most traditions, funeral rites are accompanied by music. First, is the dirge, or mourning of the dead. This then transforms into a festive song, as families and strangers come together to dance and to celebrate someone's passing from matter into eternal energy.

Grief is part of life's music, but great music includes all the notes. Grief is your personal song to sing. Turn it into an ode to joy or a lament. Your grief can be whispered or it can build to grand crescendos, but be careful not to impose your emotions on other people. Respect their art as you would want them to respect yours.

So much can be discovered when you're honest about your grief. Confounding mysteries can be better understood, and the fears you have about death might even be resolved. Listen to the way one student described the intensity of grief as a doorway to revelation:

"I heard the news of his death, and my mind went numb. Sorrow took all my strength from me. My body collapsed onto the floor. I started to moan. The moaning began softly, but grew louder until it seemed to shake the room.

"It was a sound I'd never heard before, from myself or from any living thing. It was a howl; savage, and somehow tender. It was primal and eloquent, carrying the combined force of every emotion. It grew stronger and stronger, until it finally lost its voice...until there was total stillness inside of me.

"Looking back at that moment, it seems to me that the animal and the angel had met. Flesh and spirit merged; and together, they described the truth of what I was..."

Consider that. Animal and angel: one cries out for mercy and the other offers it. Together, they create the sonic vibration of love. Without words, they tell us what we truly are.

Jolted out of its arrogance, the mind has nothing to say and no advice to give. It has no voice, no stories, and no strategies. It has no choice but to give up and admit defeat on its own battlefield.

In those moments, whatever used to seem important suddenly becomes trivial. Whatever was hidden becomes accessible. What was dreaded no longer frightens us.

In a short space of time, we may recognize the truth. We may see ourselves as we are.

We are animal and angel, both. We are matter, always in a dance with energy. Right now, we are living flesh wrapped in the eternal force of life.

Death Before Death

Your own body will die someday. This dream will end for you. Before that happens, what else do you think should end? What would you like to end? Your fear? Your doubt? Your judgments? Your pain?

The fear can end. You don't have to be afraid to receive love or to invest it. You're used to making choices based on the fear that something won't last. You know that everything ends, but you also dread endings. This can stop.

There are no beginnings without endings. There is no life without death. You can choose to be happy in that knowledge, rather than discouraged by it. You can end your doubt.

Doubt helps you to cast away old beliefs about yourself. Doubt makes it possible to detach from the main character of your story. Once doubt has freed you of illusions, you can love yourself as you are. You can be in love, always, with no doubt.

End the pain. All your anxieties about the future, about making right or wrong decisions, must end. Cultivate faith in the truth of you. End the torment that comes from your own judgments and from fearing the judgment of others.

End the imbalances. Win the war in your own mind. Put a stop to the constant conflict of ideas and see things as they are. Find a way to create equilibrium, as life does. Your mind is capable of creating its own balance by building something good out of trauma and loss. Take action. Create.

End your deceptions. Correct false impressions where you see them. Your body is a mirror for life. Your mind is the reflection, often distorting what is normal into something threatening.

Improve the way you reflect life's creative process in the private universe you call reality. Embrace all aspects of life, including death and your grief in the wake of loss.

There are many things you can allow to die, while you still exist. You can stop taking life so seriously. Laugh a little more, even in the face of tragedy. Break some habits that have no place in your dream.

Break agreements that no longer make you happy. Let go of self-pity. Lose your self-importance. Take a few bricks out of your defensive walls. Re-make old stuff. Make some new stuff. Strengthen your faith in life.

Things end. Alliances break. Expectations fail. Through it all, nurture some patience, and be kind to yourself. Be accountable for what you say and do in difficult times. In any and all conversations, see beyond the spoken words. Look beyond your own thinking. See life, pushing through matter, eager to be acknowledged.

Today, acknowledge the pain of losing someone and accept the blessings of death. Be glad that you live within your human body, feeling all there is to feel. You know you can love. Love brought precious people into your life and love will ease the heartache of losing them.

Appreciate all the beauty they left behind and the beauty that still exists in their absence, waiting to be celebrated. From this moment, you can meet every aspect of life with a willing heart. And, because you love yourself, you can survive any adversity.

Along the way, you can give comfort to a stranger. You can be a hero to the people closest to you. You can be a savior to yourself.

Human existence isn't soft and accommodating. It's shadow and light. It's filled with dangers, but also safe sanctuaries. Heartaches are inevitable but astonishing pleasures are abundant.

In your hunt for emotional food, remember that joy can be hunted and caught, just like any other prey. You can rip happiness from the jaws of misfortune, and you can keep it safe from your scary stories… because you choose to be happy, whatever the circumstance.

You choose to be happy even in illness, even in poverty. You choose to be happy when the world is urging you to be afraid. Knowing that you have a choice, why would you choose not to be happy? Knowing you have a choice, it seems the natural choice to save yourself from despair. It makes sense to rise above fear and take creative action.

You and I are still living and breathing. Life is calling us like an eager friend, bouncing a ball outside our window. It's natural for us to want to crawl out of our dark corner and play. It's hard to deny that our bodies yearn for joy.

We can find excuses to hate the world, but our hearts won't agree. We can get hooked on the taste of guilt and shame, but our dreams will suffer for it. We can identify ourselves as victims, angry and self-pitying, but then what?

When we value peace and emotional calm, we can redirect the hunter in us. We can learn to chase pleasure again, as we did in childhood. We can even choose the way we imagine reality together as a community, and as a species.

This can be your legacy and mine.

The Legacy of Smoky Mirror

There once was a young shaman who allowed himself to question his own knowledge and the wisdom of his teachers. In a moment of inspiration, he saw that matter is a mirror, bouncing light back into the universe.

He saw that his brain, made of matter, was the mirror. His mind was the reflection, rebounding light in the form of thoughts. But his thoughts were not an accurate reflection. His thoughts were guided by knowledge, easily distorted and manipulated.

In one moment, mystery gave way to revelation. By listening to his thoughts, Smoky Mirror could turn his stories toward the truth. He could clear the smoke and fog that distorted what his senses recognized as real. In that way, he could become a better reflection of life.

A smoky mirror describes the mind of every human being. It describes you, looking for a path to truth. You may sense the love inside you, but feel unable to express it authentically. You may feel that you're unable to cast a clear reflection of life.

Right now, there may be too much remorse and sorrow standing between you and your authenticity. There may be too much anger between your mind and the life that waits to embrace you.

Between you and life is a wall of noise that you built on your own. You might think this wall is necessary, but it's keeping you from seeing. It's keeping you from loving to the fullest. It's telling you not to surrender to life.

Surrendering to life means trusting whatever happens. It means treasuring the time left to us. The people we love are more than the things we notice and appreciate—more than their bodies, their minds, and their vibrant personalities. Like us, they are the current of life itself.

You, too, are life's current, which will not be stopped or impeded. Someday, if not right now, you'll want to keep loving and giving. You'll want to celebrate the legacy of those who are gone and to create a legacy of your own.

What is a legacy? A legacy is the compilation of all the experiences in your life. It is the totality of what you are, the sum of all your actions and reactions. It is the sum of your emotions. It's what you give to those who are left when you depart from your physical body.

Your awareness is your legacy, as is your authenticity, which you leave as a teaching to other human beings. When you are gone, you will leave behind all you've given to life. You will leave shared memories and your passion for life. To your family, friends, and lovers, you will leave your unconditional love.

Life. Energy. Love. Truth. Whatever you name it, you're talking about the one force that brought you into being. You're talking about the force that sustains you now and will eventually take you back again.

✳   ✳   ✳

And so we come to the end of this week's classes. I've enjoyed all the rewards of our time together and look forward to uncovering more of life's mysteries with you in the future!

Until then, take time to consider what you've learned. Recognize ideas that challenge you and allow yourself the time and effort to see them in a new light. If other ideas resonate with you, integrate them into your life.

While you grieve for what is lost, remember the one who grieves. Remember to offer yourself the same love and respect you give to the dead. If you pray for those you loved, consider what prayer can do for you, as well.

I see prayer as a song for lovers. One is calling to the other for a glimpse or for a touch. The other is responding to that call—but the two are the same. You are life, the one being, communing with yourself. You're the welcoming touch and the calming smile. You are both sides to every prayer.

You might feel that all your prayers go unheard. You might believe there is no comfort for you when someone you loved has died, but the comfort must come from you. You are the one who bestows a blessing, and you are the blessing itself.

You are the source of strength and wisdom in the wake of loss. You are the one who yearns, and you are the one who can fulfill a lifetime of yearning.

Now and forever, you are the pure potential of life. Even in your sorrow, you can choose to greet yourself each day with a hug and a kiss. You can tuck yourself into bed at night with a lullaby of tenderness and appreciation.

You can keep the love affair going between life's creative force and the astonishing creation that is you. You can do that, in your way and in your lifetime.

Class Ends